MY BROTHER'S
KEEPER
(A WARRIOR'S TALE)

MARTIN L. LAWSON

DEDICATIONS

To my wife Meko, my friend, my love, and my joy.
Smile for me. For Malia, Milan, & Maiz, may you
endeavor to be all that God has equipped you to be and
let nothing, not even yourselves, hinder you.

Seeking Marty

I once was lost, without direction.
I once was traveling without a map.
I seemed to be filled with insecurities.
I seemed to fall into every trap.

So I began "Seeking Marty"

I looked for him on a street corner.
I looked for him in a pipe.
I thought I saw him one Sunday morning.
But he disappeared later that night.

I looked for him around my homies.
They said they had not seen my friend.
They said they hope I locate Marty.
Because they're truly missing him.

I looked for him in nightclubs.
In new clothing and new shoes.
I looked in colleges, in prisons, in gangs,
In lovers, in books, and even in booze.

I looked and looked to no avail.
I looked and had no luck.
I went back to that street corner.
Because I was actually about to give up.

Then "God Almighty" spoke to me.
It was so simple I had to cry.
He said, "Why must you search the whole world over,
When Marty has been inside you all this time."

TABLE OF CONTENTS

Chapter 1

CHILDHOOD

The Early 70's"

Train up a child in the way he should go:
and when he is old, he will not depart from it.
Proverbs 22:6

M ost of my earliest memories begin in our house on 29th
street, in the Madison Valley area of Seattle Washington.
327 29th Ave E. to be exact. It was my mother(Bettye), my sis-
ter(Sheila), my brother(Carl/Doobie), myself, and my younger
sister(Natasha). My siblings and I were all two years apart with
Sheila being the oldest, then Carl, me, and finally Tash, the spoiled
baby of the bunch. My mother and Father divorced when I was
about 5years old so although I have vague memories of him in our
house my earliest clear memories of him were when my brother
and I would visit him on the weekends.

My brother Doobie and I were born in Chicago, Illinois. He
was born on March 19th 1966, and I was born on July 1st 1968. I
had two other brothers on my father's side but Doobie was the only
one with the same mother and father as me. Doobie was always
there for me for as long as I can remember.

In 1969 there was a fire in our Chicago apartment. We lost everything. My mom's sister Juanita lived in Chicago so we moved in with her for a little while until my dad could find us another place. Natasha wasn't born yet so it was just my mom, Sheila, Doobie, and I who went to stay with Juanita. After two or three months my dad hadn't found a new place so my mom decided to make a move. Mom moved us to Seattle Washington were she had two older brothers, Uncle Edgar, and Uncle Earnest. Uncle Earnest was 3years older than Juanita (who we called Tee), who was three years older than my mom. Uncle Edgar was 4years older than Uncle Earnest. My mom also had two younger brothers, James, who was 3years her junior, and Lenroe who was 6years younger than my mom, but we'll get to them later.

Uncle Edgar and Uncle Earnest helped my mom get set up when she arrived in Seattle in early 1970. We stayed with my Uncle Earnest until my mom got a job at Boeing, then we were able to move into our own house. I remember watching them build it from the ground up. 327 29th Avenue East. In spring of 1971 we moved in. It was quite an adventure for a young boy such as myself. Coming from Chicago to a brand new home on a nice street with cherry, and pear trees in our back yard. My mom did a good job, I remember being very happy.

A few months later Tee came down from Chicago and decided to stay. When my Aunt came she brought Chelsea. Chelsea was my Aunt's daughter, so that made her my first cousin on my mom's side. When we were younger I used to think Chelsea wanted to be a boy. She would follow my brother and I everywhere we went, she was only a year younger than me so she could keep up pretty good. Even when we tried to lose her.

For some reason Chelsea wouldn't do very much little girl stuff. I remember her following us thru the trails near my house. Throwing dirt bombs and fighting like one of the fellas. In fact she once gave my cousin Neil a black eye and he had to hold a potato on it for a few days, but that's another story. On one occasion my mom made me take Chelsea with me while I went to hang with my friends. This really upset me because who wants a little girl following you around when you're hanging with the fellas? I was riding Chelsea on the back of my bike when I remembered a new trick I'd learned. I'd just learned how to jump off a bike while going downhill and let it keep going. So I jumped off the bike with Chelsea on it and let her and the bike keep going. She went another 10 or 20 feet before she hit a curb and flipped over onto the parking strip. She wasn't hurt too badly but she screamed her head off. I walked her home where she told my mom and Tee what I'd done and I got in big trouble. Jumping off the bike wasn't the smartest thing to do, but I was a kid and I was mad at Chelsea so what did they expect me to do?

Growing up in the Valley was always interesting. There was always something to do. We would play football down at the Harrison school (which was later changed to Martin Luther King). We would ride our bikes all over Seattle; we'd play baseball in the streets at the end of the block. We would play hide and go seek, Tag, and a bunch of other games too numerous to name right now.

However two of my favorite games were Hot Beans and Butter, and Dark Dark Bark Bark. Dark Dark Bark Bark was pretty simple. We usually played in our basement, one of us would be blind folded and spun around, the others would then attempt to allude whoever was it while saying "Bark bark" whenever the person who was it said "Dark dark". When the person who was it caught someone, he would scream, "Bark bark", the person who was caught would then become it. Dark Dark Bark Bark was similar to Marco Polo but played on land and in the dark.

Hot Beans and butter on the other hand was more action packed and violent. One person would hide a leather belt while everyone else remained on base. Base would be a tree, a porch, or something else big enough for 4 or more people to sit on or put one hand on. Once the belt was adequately hidden the hider would yell "Hot beans and butter." Everyone would then run from the base and begin looking for the belt. The hider would give hints to the location of the belt by saying "hot" when someone was near the belt or "cold" when they moved away. When someone found the belt they would then attempt to spank anyone within range. Everyone playing, except the hider, was fair game until they made it back to the base. When everyone made it back to the base, whoever found the belt would then hide it and the whole thing would start all over again. It was always fun watching someone get cornered and spanked all the way back to the base, unless of course you were the person getting whooped. Then it was just painful, physically and mentally, since everyone else was laughing at you. My brother was one of the people you hoped didn't find the belt before you. You see Doobie was strong and fast, so he could run you down and hit you pretty hard when he caught you. When he caught someone he would get between them and the base and whoop them thoroughly until they were very sore and fortunate enough to finally make it to the base. It was against the rules to hit above the shoulders and we all usually tried to hit below the beltline, so it was all in fun. We played this game until we out grew it, because eventually no one wanted to get spanked anymore, especially not for fun.

Growing up in the Valley I always had someone to hang out with. One of the first friends I made when I moved into the "Hood," was `Hot Rod. ` Hot Rod lived with his mom and dad on the corner at the end of my block. They had a big house on the corner of 29th and Thomas, with a big back yard and a swing in a tree in the front yard. I spent a lot of time at Hot Rod's house when we were growing up. Hot Rod's dad was in an old car club so they traveled around Washington to different gatherings and events and I would often go with them. They also owned a cabin in the woods so we would go camping up there in the summer. Hot Rod's mom worked for a bank and his dad worked for the post office so his family was probably middle class. Hot Rod wasn't spoiled but he did have a lot of stuff that the rest of us were envious of, like a motorcycle. I remember when he first got it and I tried to ride it for the first time. I was about 14, which made Hot Rod 13 since he was a year younger than me. I was helping Rod cut the grass in front of his house when his dad pulled up in his blue Ford truck. This was the truck Rod's dad used to transport us to baseball practice since he was also our little league baseball coach. We played for the Astros. We even won the little league championship. That was the same year I hit a home run in the all-star game. But that's another story.

Like I said I was helping Rod cut the grass when his dad pulled up in front of the house with a Kawasaki 100 motorcycle in the back of his truck.

"Dad, who's is that?" Hot Rod yelled. "What are you doing with it?"

"Now listen here boy," this was Roger, Hot Rod's dad. He was a little country. I'm not really sure where he was from; I think it was Texas; but he had a really strong country accent.

"Ya'll come here. What ya thank?" He asked as we ran over to the truck.

"I got this here for little or nothing, and it runs good to."

"Mauday," that's what he called me even though my name was Marty. It was really Martin after Martin Luther King, but everybody called me Marty. Everyone except Roger.

"Mauday run over there and get that two-by-four so yall can get this thang outta my truck"

"Alright Roger," I yelled as I ran over to grab the two-by-four from the side of the house.

When I got back Hot Rod was already up in the truck walking the bike towards the back. I put the two-by-four in place, leaning on the truck and braced against the grass, then we began walking the bike down the board.

We were so excited, the bike didn't even seem heavy, although I found out a little later it was.

"Go head, take it round the block," Roger told Hot Rod, "See what she can do!"

Now Hot Rod was a little more experienced than I was at this kind of stuff. By having a father figure in his household he was exposed to a whole lot of stuff I missed by not having my dad at home. Not only did Hot Rod play the regular sports like football, baseball, and basketball Roger also taught him how to play golf. I tried it once or twice but I couldn't get the hang of it. By the time he was twelve Hot Rod already knew how to drive. You see his dad let him start backing the car out of the driveway as soon as he was tall enough to reach the petals and see over the windshield. He even let him drive the car around the block whenever we washed it, and Roger didn't even come with us. He was pretty cool like that. I remember wondering what my life would have been like if my dad and mom hadn't gotten a divorce. But I digress.

Hot Rod was on the bike in no time.

"Go ahead, she's yours."

"Mine?"

"Yeah son, happy birthday."

It wasn't even his birthday.

"It's not even my birthday."

"I know, but had I waited until next month it would have been gone, so happy birthday."

"Thanks dad!"

With this Hot Rod started her up.

Vrrrrrrrrrrrrrrrrrmmmmmmmmmmmmmmmm!!!!!

She started right up on the first kick, no problems at all.

"Go head, take her round the blo…"

Roger hadn't even finished his sentence before Hot Rod had sped off in the middle of the street, heading south down 29th.

"What you think Mauday? You think he likes it?"

"Yeah,"I said who wouldn't like a motorcycle for their 14th birthday.

"Yeah, I think he likes it, that's pretty cool."

"You wanna take her round next?"

"Yeah" I said without really thinking.

Like I said earlier Hot Rod was a little more experienced than I was at this kind of stuff. I had never ridden a motorcycle. The closest I'd come to driving was starting the car up in the winter, so it would be warmed up for my mom when she got ready to go to work. But I figured if Rod could do it, being younger than me, how hard could it be.

"Awright you can go next when Rod gets back."

"Cool ," I said, the excitement turning to concern.

By now I could hear Hot Rod coming up the block.

Vrrrrrrrrrmmm, vrrrrrrrrrrrrrrrrrrmmmmmmmmmmmm, vvvvvrrrrrrrrrrrrrrrrrrrrrmmmmmmmmmmmmmmmmmmmmmm."

Hot Rod had ridden all the way around the block and he was now on his way up the hill heading straight for Roger and I, who were now standing in the middle of the street.

"Man that's live," He said as he pulled up next to us, hitting the brakes with a screech.

"Let Mauday have a try now," Roger said to Rod who was all grins.

"Alright" Hot Rod said as he put the gears in neutral and climbed off the bike standing next to it holding it for me.

The motorcycle now seemed a lot taller than I remembered it. I climbed on and gave it a little gas. 'I can do this I thought'.

"It's just like riding a dirt bike. Here are your gears," Hot Rod said pointing to a lever next to my left foot. "This is the front brake, but don't use it," he said. "Use your back brakes, that way you won't flip over. They're right there by your right foot, and here is the clutch."

He said pointing to the lever on the handlebars next to my left hand.

"Squeeze it before you put it into gear and let it out slowly as you give it gas."

"Alright, I got it," I said, trying to look like I knew more than I actually did.

I gave it a little gas.

15

Then I put it in first gear.

I gave it a little more gas.

Then I popped the clutch.

That's the last thing I remember.

When I came to, Roger and Hot Rod were standing over me Yelling.

"Mauday, Mauday, you alright? Wake up."

I opened my eyes and looked around.

The motorcycle was lying next to me on its side with the back wheel spinning.

I later found out from Hot Rod that I had given it to much gas and let go of the clutch too quickly. This caused the bike to pop a wheelie and throw me off the back.

I banged my head on the concrete knocking me unconscious for about a minute.

Thankfully the bike landed next to me instead of on me.

So I wasn't damaged very much (I wasn't even bleeding), and Hot Rod's motorcycle wasn't damaged either.

I did give Rod and his dad a good scare though.

I did eventually learn how to ride that motorcycle, and we used to take it up to the cabin Roger owned up in Granite Falls, Washington and ride it through the trails. I learned quickly and I never fell again after that.

I had a bunch of other friends in the Valley as well. The very first person I met when I moved to the Valley was Brian. Brian was also a year younger than I was, but he was a lot bigger than me.

Brian was bigger than all of my friends

Brian was mixed like Hot Rod, meaning his dad was black and his mom was white. But Brian didn't look like Hot Rod, Brian looked Hawaiian, or Samoan. Whoever those big guys are that live on the islands, and grow real big. That's how big Brian was.

I stood about four foot-ten at the age of 14 and Brian stood head and shoulders over me.

He had to be about a foot taller than me. And he was heavyset. He wasn't what I would call fat, but he was large. Like a linebacker.

Brian lived in a house behind my house. You could see Brian's house from my backyard. We would take this route through the bushes in our back yard to get to Brian's backyard. This was much faster than going around the block on the sidewalk.

My brother and I could often be found at Brian's house. You see Brian was an only child, and Brian was spoiled.

Growing up, it seemed like Brian had every toy we saw on TV. As soon as it came out he had it. He had Intellivision, Colecovision, Atari, Atari 6400. He had all of the Star Wars figures, including Boba Fet. He had the Star Wars x-wing fighters, and the Darth Vader ship. We would make them fight against the Battle star Gallactica spaceships. These weren't the cheap ships either. These were the ones that had the little plastic missiles that shot out when you pushed the button.

He also had the NFL football game where the whole board would vibrate and your men would move and block each other. We would stay over Brian's house for hours. Plus his mom made the best popcorn I have ever tasted. She would put meat tenderizer, seasoning salt or something on it. I still put seasoning salt on my popcorn to this day because of that.

Brian loved my mom's fried chicken though. He would use all of his allowance to buy a couple pieces from me whenever my mom made it. He used to get $.25 every time he made his own cereal so he usually had a couple of dollars on him.

We were pretty good friends. But we hadn't always been close.

I remember one time when I was about 8 years old we were all in front of my house playing kickball. Actually Brian and I weren't playing because my brother and sister said we were too small (or too young in Brian's case). But any way, Brian and I were watching my brother, my sister, her friend Bridget, Bridget's brother Dawayne, a kid named Cedric, and a few other kids I didn't really know play kick ball in front of my house.

Kickball is sort of like baseball, except there is no bat, and it's played with a big rubber ball which is rolled at the person whose turn it is to kick. He/she then kicks the ball and runs around the bases until he makes it back to home plate. He/she is out if someone catches the ball in the air, or if someone hits them with the ball while they are off the base.

Brian and I couldn't play so I was throwing dirt bombs at the players as they ran by us.

Brian was throwing rocks.

When my brother got up to the plate I stopped to watch because he kicked a home run the last time he was up. So I was interested in seeing if he could do it again. He asked for his pitch to be slow and bouncy, and then he kicked it. The ball soared high and fast, all the way across the street into the neighbor's yard. While the other team scrambled for the ball, my brother was flying around the bases. I was transfixed on my brother as he came around third base and began heading home where Brian and I were standing.

And then, out of the corner of my eye I saw Brian hurl half a brick.

"You're out," Brian said as the brick collided with the side of my brother's head.

Everything stopped for a moment. It seemed like slow motion as my brother grabbed his head in mid stride and began to yell. Blood was pouring from his head and he was yelling like he had stepped on a nail, or been shot or something.

I turned to ask Brian why he had done that and I barely caught a glimpse of him as he rounded the corner on his way home. He had started running as soon as he heard Doobie

yell. He was half way home with my sister and Bridget on his tail. They didn't catch him though. That was the fastest I ever saw Brian move.

We took my brother in the house and my mom took him to the hospital where he had to get five stitches. After they got home my brother went and lay on the couch to watch cartoons. I was really mad at Brian for hurting my brother. Then I heard a knock on the door. When I looked through the window next to the door to see who it was it was Brian.

"What do you want," I said, with an attitude thinking 'the nerve of this guy coming over here after hitting my brother in the head with a brick.'

"I just wanted to say I'm sorry, it was an accident" Brian said as he handed me a package.

"And I wanted to give Doobie this."

I looked into the bag and it was about fifteen candy bars. Snickers, Milkyway, Almond Joy, and some bubbliscous bubble gum.

I looked at Brian and he looked genuinely sorry.

"O.k." I said, "I'll give this to him" "And I'll tell him you're sorry"

"Thanks Marty," "You guys come over when he feels better; I just got some new cartridges for Atari."

"Alright, I'll tell him" I said as I closed the door.

"Who was that?" Doobie asked.

"It was Brian, he said he was sorry for hitting you in the head, and he sent you some candy" I said as I handed my brother ten candy bars.

I wasn't as mad at Brian after that, but I didn't go back over his house until my brother felt better and we went together.

I remember another incident I had with Brian when we were a little older.

I think I was about ten when Brian and I got into our first and only fight. Now like I said, I wasn't very big. In fact I was smaller than most of the kids my age when I was growing up, so I guess I may have developed something called a little man complex. Since I was small I was quick to fight anyone who got in my face. Regardless of how big they were. Because of this I ended up getting in a lot of fights while I was growing up. I was small, but I was something people down south would call, 'Cock strong'. That meant I was a pretty strong guy, in spite of my size. I really can't remember losing many fights, except to my brother and older sister, but they don't count.

So anyway Brian and I were at odds about something one day, I'm not really sure what, but we were arguing in my backyard.

"So what, boy." I said.

"Shut up, before I kick you in the face." Brian said.

"You aint gonna kick nobody in the face, you better go home before you make me hurt you". I told him.

"You can't hurt nobody boy. You need to go lay down before I really get mad and smash you."

By this time Brian's dad had heard us arguing and came to the edge of our yard to see what was going on.

"What are you two fighting about"? He asked us

Neither one of us really remembered what the topic was, we just knew we were mad at each other.

"He told me to shut up or he was gonna kick me in the face".

"So what" said Brian who for some reason seemed to get braver when his dad showed up.

"I will kick you in the face, and you're lucky I don't smash you like a bug, little boy."

'LITTLE?'

Oh no, I know he didn't just call me little.

I was on him before he knew what happened. I remember charging him at full speed and trying to knock him on the ground. But as you remember Brian was a lot bigger than me so my attack didn't have its desired effect. Instead we just began to wrestle and push each other back and forth. Somehow Brian ended up behind me and he was trying to give me a bear hug. It was starting to hurt and I didn't know what to do. I also remember his dad who wasn't making a move towards breaking us up; he was just kind of watching to see what would happen. Me on the other hand, I was getting lightheaded.

So in a last ditch effort, I punched my right fist over my right shoulder hoping to hit something.

POW!!!

I connected. I had hit Brian Square in the nose.

"AAHHHHHHHHHHH" He said as he let go of me.

"AAAHHHHHHHHHHHHHHHHHHHHHHHHHH" He said again, this time louder and with more passion when he saw the blood ooz out of his nose.

"Daaaaaaaddddddddddddd".

By this time Brian was holding his nose and running home. I still remember his dad looking at me. Not in anger but in a kind of awe. Like, 'How did he do that?"

I watched them go home then I went in the house feeling pretty good about myself.

Kind of like Napoleon. He was a little guy to but he did big things. I wonder if he had a little man's complex. Maybe that's why he tried to conquer the world.

Anyway Brian and I never fought again after that. At least not in anger. We wrestled a lot, but I think that day we developed a certain amount of respect for one another.

Around the fifth or six grade the Kilgores moved into the hood. They moved in on the North side of Madison on 28th street. Two houses down from the Watsons. The Watsons were Bruce and Andre. The Kilgores were Mark and Shawn.

The Kilgores were mixed children. Their Dad, Carl was black and their mom, Pam was white. Their mom and dad had gotten a divorce before they moved to the valley so they lived with their mom and her mom. Mark was the oldest, he was my age, in fact we would go on to graduate from Garfield High School in the same year, 1986. Shawn was a year younger than I was. He was Hot Rod's age. They would graduate from Garfield in 1987. Mark and Shawn Kilgore were two of the most peculiar and interesting children I had ever met in my childhood. They were both extremely spoiled, and extremely competitive with one another. Their house would be one of the first houses I visited the day after Christmas (Brian's would be the other). They along with Brian would get incredible amounts of gifts on Christmas, but because there were two of them, their take would be double. Of course they would always receive the standard clothing, pants, socks, shirts, coats, hats, etc…all in the latest style, but they would also receive the latest toys in abundance, times two. If Mark got the newest Atari 5200, Shawn got Colecovision. If Mark got a bike, Shawn got a bike. They both got their own television to play their own video games in their own room. The room situation was something major in itself to me coming from a household with three other siblings and having always shared my room with my brother. They didn't just get the normal run of the mill kids' stuff, they got top of the line hand held video games, racetracks, stereo systems, and in high school their own cars. But I'm getting ahead of myself.

As kids Mark and Shawn would compete and argue about almost everything, from whether the light should be on or off in the living room to who I was there to visit. They seldom fought but their arguments were sites to behold.

"Get out of my room PUNK!!!"

"Make me"

"You're stupid, that's why you don't have any friends"

"What are you talking about? Marty's here to see me"

"No he's not"

"Yes he is, aren't you Marty?"

At this point I would be thrust into the middle of the discussion but I was wise enough not to answer directly.

"What???" I'd say, feigning confusion.

Then they were right back at it.

"You're stupid, if he's here to see you, why is he in my room?"

"Because you stink like shit and we wanted to see what the problem is"

"Ooooohhhh!!!!, MOM MARK IS CUSSING, he said SHIT"

"You do stink like shit cause mom always has to make you take a bath"

"That's your upper lip"

"Your teeth look like yellow chicklets"

"Your breath is so bad your teeth are melting"

"Your breath is so bad your tongue be trying to escape, that's why mom is going to get you braces so your tongue can't escape."

"Whatever, yo momma likes it."

"Ooooooooohhh, mom!!!"

This would go on for hours until they got tired or Pam broke it up. I would just sit back, laughing my head off the whole time.

This was a daily routine with Mark and Shawn but you learned to get used to it and after that it was just very entertaining.

Another of my early childhood friends was Greg. Greg lived on 29th street as well, about a block and a half from our house. Greg was a year older than I was. While we were growing up we kind of thought Greg was a pathological liar. He always seemed to have either experienced everything we talked about doing or he knew someone who had. Not only was he a "Me Too"; meaning if you said you had done something, or you were going to do something, he would say "Me Too," he was also constantly contradicting any plans or ideas we would come up with.

"Let's go to Madison beach and go swimming" my brother Doobie said one sunny summer afternoon.

"Why", responded Greg "It's too crowded there, we should go to the Slew".

Now the Slew was a little secluded spot in the Arboretum where Lake Washington went under highway 520 to connect to Lake Union. Madison beach was a public beach in the Madison Park area of the Valley.

"Yeah" said Brian, who was a heavy kid so he didn't like people seeing him with his shirt off. "Let's go to the Slew, there's a rope swing there".

"Ahh B, you just don't want nobody to see your belly" Doobie responded.

"Plus we want it to be crowded because that's where all the girls are," this from Hot Rod who was the pretty boy of the crew. This being the late 70's when light skin was in and darker brothers like myself had a hard time competing.

"So what," Said Greg, who was even darker than I was, "Don't nobody feel like tripping with all those people trying to find a spot on the beach. Plus there be dogs and stuff there."

"There be dogs at the Slew too, plus there aint any lifeguards at the Slew. Who's going to save you if your big ass head starts sinking?" This from my brother Dobbie who had actually saved me from drowning once in a public pool, but that's another story. "You're just scared of girls, Blacula"

"You're stupid, aint nobody scared of girls."

"Whatever," Dobbie responded, "then let's go to Madison."

This discussion went on for about ten to fifteen minutes with us trying to decide which beach we should go to. Brian and Greg pushed for the Slew and Doobie and Hot Rod pushed for Madison beach. I really didn't care which beach we went to. They both had their pros and cons, and I was more interested in making sure everybody got to go so we could have more fun.

"Let's go to the Slew" I said when I got tired of them going back and forth. "We can go to Madison tomorrow. That way we can jump off the bridges and they have a nude beach over by the Slew."

Although it wasn't really a nude beach just somewhere women would come to sunbathe topless this peaked everyone's attention.

"Yeah, I saw some people doing it over there once" Greg stated trying to strengthen his case for going to the Slew. "I was hiding in the bushes and they didn't even know I was there."

"I barely know you're here now" said Doobie. "Get out of the shade; stand in the sun so I can see you, before you started talking I thought you went home."

"You're dumb" Greg replied weakly.

"You're dumb, that's why you're twelve years old and still in the fifth grade."

"My birthday is late, that's why I started late."

"Whatever, Brainiac."

"Your MAMA!!!" This is what someone usually said when he was getting ranked on and didn't have a good enough response.

"OHHHHHHHHHHHHHHHHH" all the cosigners said like he had gotten in a major blow.

But a good ranker would keep his composer and not be thrown off by this tactic.

"Your mama, she only got one leg talking about she can beat PELE in soccer, She aint got no arms talking about she's on the United States gymnastics team with Nadia Comaneci, your whole family be lying. Your mom's boyfriend thinks he invented peanut butter and that's all he eats, that's why he looks like Mr. Planter the peanut dude."

"AAAHHHHHHHHHH, he killed you" we said as we all fell out laughing.

"Greg I'd quit if I was you" Hot Rod said.

"I know" said Brian.

"Whatever" said Greg, pretty much conceding.

Although my brother would rank on Greg none of us wanted to fight him. He was one of the toughest dudes in the valley. His older brother Maurice was a kick boxer who would go on to become a world champion so he would rough Greg up and try all of these new moves on him. This made Greg tough and there weren't to many people our age who could handle him in a fight.

"Let's go" I said, jumping on my bike. "The last one to the Slew is a rotten egg.

This was during the late seventies before the razor blades in your Halloween candy scare, before the cyanide in the Tylenol scare, before all of those kids disappeared in Atlanta, before the internet and all of the concerns that came with it. So we were usually allowed to roam freely throughout our neighborhood without supervision as long as we were home before the street lights came on.

We would ride our bikes for miles during the summer. To the University of Washington campus. To Seward Park. And all over the Valley. Which in our understanding extended south to Union street, north to Valley street, west to 23rd Avenue and East to Lake Washington. We would ride all throughout the Arboretum trails and as we got older we would ride all the way to the bike trails at Green lake or to Seward Park. Life seemed so much simpler and safer back then.

When we arrived at the Slew we got off and walked our bikes through the nude beach hoping to catch a glimpse of some part of the female anatomy that we weren't accustomed to seeing, but we were all curious about. I had seen the female anatomy a number of times when I stayed with my dad on the weekends. He had a subscription to Playboy so he would have an extensive collection of magazines that my brother and I would sneak peeks at whenever we got the chance. The women at the beach however would see us coming and turn over so there was nothing really to see but some flat butts and exposed backs which really didn't do much for us at all. We did catch a fleeting peek at a breast once when one of the women stood up to dress.

"Oh, did you see that?"

"See what?"

"That titty over there."

"Where, Where?"

"Shhh, Brian be quiet, she'll hear you. Right there next to that tree. She's putting her bra on now."

"Why didn't you tell me."

"I did, it just happened so fast, she did have big titties though."

"I know I saw her titties last time I was here with my brother, she was coming out of the water though and I saw both of them. Then she came over and said hi."

"Shut up Greg, you be lying. You aint never even seen a titty. Your Mom don't even have any titties, she had to borrow the neighbor's titty to breast feed you. That's why you're so black. Your neighbor is from Africa. That's why we don't be understanding half the stuff you be saying."

My brother could go on like this for hours. He would rank until someone either wanted to fight or cry. But there were three people in the valley who you just didn't want to start ranking on you, Shawn Kilgore, Butchie Brown, and Dennis Lee Beard. These guys would come up with ranks so ridiculously funny your face would hurt from laughing so much. But life isn't always funny. I would live to see two of these guys buried. One from an overdose, and one from a motorcycle accident, the third would recover from crack cocaine addiction like me to go on to get married and have a family.

Life, hopefully you live and you learn.

We were young and free. Oblivious to the trials of life that stood before us. Of the five of us that rode to the Slew that day four would end up going to prison, one would die from four gunshot wounds to the back, one would survive five gunshot wounds, one would be addicted to cocaine for ten years, one would be in prison as I write this book and only one would escape the maze of life seemingly unscathed.

"Last one in the water has to do twenty five pushups."

We swam that day enjoying friendship, life and freedom. Until my brother got hurt.

"Watch this." Doobie said as he grabbed the rope preparing to swing out over the water.

"I can go out further than everybody."

He grabbed the rope and proceeded to back up to get a running start. He didn't realize that the further back he went the lower he held on to the rope. So when he ran forward and grabbed the rope to swing out over the water his knees didn't clear the ground.

"AAAHHHHH, help me, help me." Doobie screamed

He had scraped his knee on a big rock and he had a huge gash in his leg.

"AAAHHHHH, heeeelllppp."

My brother wasn't very tolerant of pain.

"Doob, what happened?" I asked after running over to him.

"Aaaahhh, look at my leg."

Blood was beginning to stream down his leg and you could see the white flesh under the skin that had been peeled back. It looked like it was deep enough to see the bone.

"Ow, ow , ow ,ow,"

"It's going to be alright Doob, just calm down. You guys come over here, Brian bring me that towel."

With some effort we were able to wrap my brother's leg pretty tight so I could ride him home on the back of my bike. Hot Rod rode his bike while pulling my brother's bike with one hand. Needless to say my mom was pretty upset when she saw how bad Doobie was cut. He ended up getting about fourteen stitches in his leg to close the wound, and we ended up having to sneak to the Slew after that because my mother didn't think it was safe for us to be so far from help, and around water without a life guard present. But we were young and unaware of the risks involved in what we were doing plus we thought our parents were just old, un-cool, and trying to prevent us from having all of the fun we deserved to have. So we continued to grow and run and play enjoying youth and the benefits included in childhood. I look at my children now and I try to prepare them for a world that isn't always glad to see them, and doesn't always have their best interests in mind. A world that can sometimes be unbalanced, and biased, favoring one group of individuals over another, or distorting the value of what is true and right for personal prosperity. A world where some acquire wealth at the expense of others. As an adult I better understand the boundaries set by my mother and the concerns she expressed. But when you're young your attention span normally isn't that long. So life goes on.

In 1978 my mother's younger brother James moved to Seattle from Chicago. Uncle James was about four years younger than my mom, who was about five years younger than her sister Juanita. Altogether my Grandmother Addie Lee Morgan had seven children Auntie Clementine was the oldest, then Uncle Edgar, Juanita, Uncle Earnest, my mom, Uncle James, and Uncle Len who was the baby of the bunch. They were raised in a little town called Lena Mississippi and all of them except Clementine migrated north during the 60s.

When Uncle James arrived in 1978 I remember being over Tee's house when a big U-haul truck pulled up in front of the house. My Uncle James was driving the U-haul and his wife Auntie Lois was in the passenger seat. I can only remember meeting Uncle James and Auntie Lois one time prior to that night, and that was one year when my mom took us to Chicago. It was in the summer because I remember us going down to the beach on Lake Michigan, and even though it was hot we couldn't go in the water because for some reason the fish were dying and washing up on the beach. The beach was full of dead fish, everywhere you turned. For some reason I don't remember it being a big deal to Uncle James, just a normal occurrence in the waters of Lake Michigan.

Uncle James and Auntie Lois had two children. James Cornelius Morgan, and Tiffany Morgan. James Cornelius (who we called Neil) was one year younger than I was, the same age as Tee's daughter Chelsea. Tiffany was four years younger than me. I first met Neil and Tiffany on that same trip to Chicago. It was near the fourth of July because we were catching fire flies then putting them in pop cans with fire crackers and blowing up the cans along with the insects. We were bored and told by the adults to go outside and amuse ourselves so that is what we were doing. When we tired of exterminating insects we began to look for other ways to entertain ourselves. My brother suggested kickball which most of us agreed upon, except for my sister Sheila and Neil who decided to play Frisbee with a flat pop can which had been run over by a car. Everything was fine and we were all enjoying ourselves until Sheila threw the pop can Frisbee and Neil tried to catch it. I don't know if it was the velocity at which my sister threw the can, or the lack of coordination possessed by Neil who was around seven years old at this time. Whatever the cause, Neil didn't catch the can. Instead the can caught him right between the eyes.

"Aagghghghghgh mommmmmmmmmmm!!!!!! Neil cried in terror at the top of his lungs.

"Mommy, AAAaaaaaghHHHHHHHHHHhhhhhh mommy!!!! This as he was now running into the house with blood running down his face.

A sight like that can be pretty frightening for a group of children so we were all understandably a little shaken.

"What happened?" Doobie asked as we ran over to Sheila who was standing as if she was in shock.

"Sheila, what happened?" Dobbie asked again

"He didn't catch the Frisbee" Sheila responded

"SHEILA GWEN" we heard my mom yell from the house.

"Sheila Gwen, come here right now."

Now we knew there was going to be trouble. My mom only used our middle names when she was really angry.

Sheila headed to the house with us close behind her. We were eager to find out what happened, but we didn't want to get caught up in the backlash. Sometimes if someone got in big enough trouble everyone there would get a whipping, the one who did it, because he did it, and the ones who were there because they didn't stop him. This sounded like one of those `everybody is in trouble` situations, so we were playing it somewhat cautious.

We didn't know why Sheila was being called. It could be because she was the one who threw the pop can Frisbee, or it could be because she was the oldest of us and usually left in charge.

"Sheila!!! What happened to this boy" My mom asked my sister when Sheila finally, reluctantly, reached the house.

"We was playing and he accidentally got hit in the face."

"What were you playing?" Mom asked.

"We was playing Frisbee." Sheila replied.

"Frisbee?" My mom asked. "How in the hell did a Frisbee cut that boy like that?"

By this time Neil's was being tended to by Auntie Lois, and after washing all of the blood off of his face you could see a nice sized cut directly between his eyes. A fraction of an inch in either direction and he could have lost an eye. Neil had stop hollering and was now complaining as Auntie Lois dabbed an alcohol covered towel on the wound.

"SSSSSthhhh, ow ow ow! Mom that hurts."

"I know baby" Auntie Lois said. "I'm almost done"

Meanwhile after assuring ourselves that Neil wasn't seriously injured, we tuned back into the interrogation of my sister.

Now being the oldest child of a single parent meant a lot of responsibility was placed on Sheila's shoulders. She was a part time babysitter, cook, tutor, and housekeeper. I later wondered as an adult if she had been somewhat robbed of a real childhood by being thrust into the role of caretaker for the rest of us so early in her life. But being a pre-teen at this time, and having learned how to avoid giving exact answers to questions that may incriminate her, she was still being questioned by my mom as to how a Frisbee could put such a dent in Neil's forehead.

"If you didn't have a Frisbee, how in the hell were you guys playing Frisbee?"

My mom asked, the irritation beginning to rise in her voice.

"We were playing with other flat things." Sheila replied meekly.

"What kind of flat things," my mother asked, tiring from this line of questioning.

"A pop can."

"A POP CAN?" my mother yelled. "You threw a flat pop can at that boys head? Are you crazy? Girl, don't you know you could have put that boy's eye out?"

Sheila wisely didn't respond. This was a rhetorical question and she probably would have hurt her position more if she had answered. A yes answer would have been met with, "Than why did you do it?" A no answer could have been met with "you didn't know a flat, jagged piece of metal could cut that boy?" So Sheila just averted her eyes and looked real sad and concerned.

"He's okay Bettye" said my uncle James. It's just a little cut, and it was an accident.

This probably saved Sheila's butt, plus the fact that we were visiting from out of town. So the whole idea was for everybody to enjoy themselves on this trip. That definitely meant more leniencies for us. We could be a little louder, and a little rowdier. So Sheila was spared a severe butt whooping and we went back outside with instructions to avoid any games that involved cans or throwing.

After my uncle James and his family arrived my extended family seemed to get closer. All of my Aunts, Uncles and cousin were always present at every holiday gathering and Christmas, Easter, and Thanksgivings were the biggest family gathering days of the year. We would all meet at a designated house; ours, my aunt's, or my uncle's, and we would commence to celebrate the holiday and family. These were some of the best parts of my childhood, being surrounded by loved ones in a loving environment. Everyone would contribute something to the meal for that day which usually meant that we had to have two or three tables to hold all of the turkey, mashed potatoes, red beans and rice, plain rice, candied yams, greens, black eyed peas, fried chicken, baked chicken, roast beef, green beans, salads, cakes, sweet potato pies, and other goodies and desserts too numerous to name here. One of my mom's famous desserts was her coconut layer cake. I remember being in the kitchen watching her make it from scratch. It was as if she had been making it all of her life. She didn't need a recipe; she would just add certain ingredients as they were needed in the exact amount that was needed. This was especially fascinating to me because the cakes would always come out just right, and taste the same as the one before it. We would sit around the kitchen waiting to lick the batter out of the bowl, and off the spoon my mom used to stir the batter before pouring it into the cast iron skillet she baked the layers in. The whole house would be filled with the sweet smell of cake. Even though I would one day become a chef, I never did learn how to bake from scratch like my mom.

At the family gatherings we would all assemble and joke and play, laugh and eat. Grateful for another chance to see that cousin we hadn't seen since the last holiday, or "Ooh, and Aahh" over the latest addition to the family. The adults would sit around talking about the state of the world and what they would do differently if they were in power. They would talk about what their kids are doing now, the good and the bad, as we tried to stay out of the field of vision when we heard our name mentioned. We didn't want to have to deal with the hugs and embarrassing compliments that accompanied great accomplishments, or deal with the hard looks and lectures that went along with our deeds that fell short of what was expected of us. If the deed was bad enough it was not uncommon to receive a lecture or a beating from several aunts and uncles. My mom and her siblings were close and they helped each other in any way they could, that included disciplining us. This created a familial bond that has passed the test of time, drugs, prison, death, and disease. I always feel a bit of sympathy for families who have allowed disputes over money or material things to come between them. Money comes and goes, clothing goes in and out of style, cars get old and depreciate, but family is forever.

Since my family was so close they all ended up at the same house of worship, Mount Zion Baptist Church. I remember going to a small church on 19th and Madison in my very early days. Mount Zion has since grown to become one of the largest and most influential churches in the Northwest. Led by God and pastored by the Reverend Dr. Samuel Barry McKinney, Mount Zion played an important part in the development of the black community, and community as a whole in the Seattle area.

My mom and my aunts, Juanita and Auntie Lois were in the main sanctuary choir. My cousin Chelsea was in the children's choir, my uncle James was on the security team. My siblings and I would just sit in the balcony with the rest of the young people and listen to Rev. McKinney preach in his deep baritone voice. Church was not an option for us growing up. We would be instructed to "Get up" "Eat breakfast" and "Get ready for Sunday school," in that order. It was not a request and we knew my mom was serious when she said, "Let's go." I didn't know it at the time but my future wife's family was also very active at Mt. Zion Baptist Church. I learned a great deal about God in those early Sunday school lessons and those booming sermons. I was baptized at Mt. Zion as a child and I knew a little about God early on. Although I went on to make some major mistakes, and do some things that were completely contrary to how I was raised, I do believe that those seeds, dealing with God and family, that were planted in me way back in my youth are the very reason that I am still here today. Even though I didn't understand it then, I now know that God has always had a plan for my life.

One of my favorite activities, while growing up, was little league football. I started playing at the age of seven even though the youngest age group was 8 and 9 year olds. This group was the 89ers and it was the youngest of five team leagues that went up to the Gil Dobies who were 14 and 15 years old. For some reason I played my first year of football with Rainier Green, a team that practiced in South Seattle. I'm not sure why I played for that team but I know I didn't like it very much. The next year I played for the Central Area Youth Association, or C.A.Y.A. The C.A.Y.A. teams practiced at Garfield High School which was about a mile and a half from my house. I liked playing for C.A.Y.A. much better because many of my friends from the neighborhood played for them as well. I played running back on offense and cornerback on defense and I was pretty good. I wasn't the fastest kid on the field but I wasn't the slowest either. I was usually somewhere in the top five or top ten fastest on each team I played on and if I didn't start I still got a lot of playing time. One year we even won the championship. We'd gone to the championship before but this was the first year we actually won it. I remember spending the night over my coach's house for a team sleepover the day before the game. We went over plays and planned our strategy for the next day and then we sat around listening to Kurtis Blow's new album. These were the good ole days in football. After little league many of my teammates went on to high school with me.

When I wasn't playing football I was usually fighting someone. For some reason I got into a lot of fights in my youth. I was kind of small for my age and people would sometimes think that they could mistreat me because of my size. Early on I learned that if you let someone mistreat you once they would probably do it again, so I was quick to fight anyone who looked at me funny, regardless of their size. I learned to defend myself from fighting my older brother and sister. Doobie and I would fight over almost anything and Sheila was often left in charge of us so her method of instruction was usually a punch or a push. On one occasion I came home from school after being jumped by a boy and his older brother. Sheila walked me right back up to their house telling me that I was going to either fight her or fight the boys. We went to their house and called out to them but they wouldn't come out so we eventually left.

My sister wasn't the only tough girl in our neighborhood. In the fourth and fifth grade I went to Stevens Middle School with two girls from my neighborhood who nobody in the school wanted to fight. They were bigger than most of the boys in our grade and they walked around the school like they owned it. One of my friends ended up liking one of the girls so she and I were cool. I would walk over to her house with him after school so that they could kiss and hang out. I was the third wheel but that was common in those days. You needed a friend around for those kind of moments.

I actually got my first girlfriend after getting into a fight with her at school. Her name was Vanessa and I don't know if we fought because we liked each other or if we began to like each other after we fought. Whatever the case might have been we fought. I won, and soon afterwards we started hanging out as boyfriend and girlfriend. In those days the boy would ask the girl if she wanted to "go with him" which meant "go out with him". So one day, weeks after our fight, I asked Vanessa if she wanted to go with me and she said yes. Vanessa lived a few blocks from the school so she would stop by a store on her way to school and steal boxes of candy which she then shared with the other kids. This made her pretty popular at our elementary school. After we became boyfriend and girlfriend she would bring me candy almost every day and I would walk her home after school. When we got to her house I would kiss her gently on the lips and head home. The kiss on the lips was a big deal for us until one day we were walking home with another couple who were a year younger than we were. When they kissed they opened their mouths and touched tongues. Vanessa and I were shocked as we watched these two kiss goodbye. This was definitely kissing on another level. After kissing for what seemed like several minutes they stopped and said goodbye. I felt like I was missing something. What was this new opened mouth kissing all about? Vanessa and I hung out for the rest of the school year but we never did take our kissing to level that we witnessed that day. I would have to wait another year before I learned to kiss with my mouth open.

In the sixth grade my mom enrolled us in a Catholic school called Saint Mary's. I liked Saint Mary's a lot even though my mom gave the principal permission to paddle us when we misbehaved. I was called to the office on several occasions to receive a couple of swats after doing something in school that I had no business doing. The paddle hurt but at least when it was over you could go back to what you were doing without the threat of lingering consequences. So when I was presented with the option of a paddle or notifying my mom I took the paddle.

In the sixth grade my teacher took part of our class to California for a field trip during spring break. We were given a couple of months to sell candy as a fundraiser and then we took a train from Seattle to Anaheim, California. I remember being in the dome car, at night on the way to California, and having my first open mouth kiss with a girl named Tracy. Tracy wasn't officially my girlfriend I just thought she was cute. The dome car was one of those moments when all of your friends were hooking up with someone so you had to hook up with someone as well.

In California we hung out in Anaheim for a few days and went to some of the local attractions like Lion Country Safari. We also went to downtown Los Angeles where three of my friends wandered off from the rest of the group. My teacher and the chaperone were frantic and didn't know what to do. We searched around downtown for a few hours and then headed back to the motel where we were staying. When we got back to the motel we were surprised to find Roy, Eric, and Michael swimming in the motel pool as if nothing had happened. It turns out that Roy had family in LA so they took a bus to their house and hung out with his family for a while before having one of his uncles drive them back to the motel. My teacher was relieved that they were safe but pissed that they had wandered off so she made them stay in the room while the rest of us had free time to swim. This trip was one of the highlights of my childhood and I remember how good it felt to be exposed to different environments. I believe that trip developed a love of traveling within me that is still present to this day.

Back at home I returned to the normal daily routines. Life as a kid was not always fun and games. One of the things I disliked most was when my mom would send me to the store to get something with food stamps. Although my mom worked for Boeing we still were eligible for a little government assistance. This meant that every month we would get a huge block of government cheese, peanut butter, and boxes of powdered milk. The cheese and the peanut butter weren't so bad but I could not stand the powdered milk. If you've ever tried to drink powdered milk or use it in your cereal you would know exactly what I mean. We would also get an allotment of food stamps that came in books with different monetary denomination. There were $20, $10, $5, and $1 stamp denominations. My mom would often send me to the neighborhood store with a book of stamps to get some milk, bread, eggs, or sugar when she sent me to get her cigarettes. I disliked buying the cigarettes just as much as I disliked spending the food stamps. As I got older I would hide her cigarettes and when my sister Sheila began to smoke I would throw her cigarettes away when I found them.

My mom was unable to continue paying tuition for us at St. Mary's after my seventh grade so I attended Washington Middle School for my eighth grade year. Washington was a public school so after going to Saint Mary's for the sixth and seventh grade Washington was a huge change. We had skating parties in the gym almost every week and if the school didn't sponsor a skating party we would go out to Skate King in Bellevue. A number of my friends from Elementary school and football went to Washington so I tended to get into more trouble than I had at Saint Mary's. I ended up getting expelled from school in the eighth grade for being in the wrong place at the right time. I didn't really do anything but I was with two friends who did something they shouldn't have so I was guilty by association. My grades were good so I still received my eighth grade diploma but I wasn't able to attend the graduation ceremony. My mom was very disappointed and I was angry at being expelled for something I didn't do but the principal had made his decision and there was nothing I could do to change it. I was headed for high school and although I had a tendency to get into trouble when I was around my friends I hoped that I would be assigned to Garfield where I knew most of my friends would be attending.

Me, Sheila, Tash, Chelsea, & Carl

Micheal & Carl at Mt. Zion

Mom & Auntie Lois
1968

Sheila, Carl, Me
& Chelsea with
unknown dude

Sheila, Neil,
Carl, & Me

Tee

40

Chapter 2

COMING OF AGE

*For at the window of my house I looked
through my casement, and beheld among the
simple ones, I discerned among the youths, a
young man void of understanding.*
Proverbs 7:6-7

The Mis-education of Martin

In June of 1986 I graduated from Garfield High School in Seattle, Washington. Although I graduated from Garfield, I hadn't started high school there. I started high school at Roosevelt high school in the north end of Seattle. This was when the Seattle school district was bussing a lot of students out of their neighborhoods in an effort to make the schools more 'integrated.' So I ended up at Roosevelt, which was a primarily white school. I had problems there from the beginning. I once was cornered in the bathroom by a group of five white boys. I ended up fighting one of them. The kid got me in a headlock and he thought he had me until I punched my right hand up and caught him square on the nose. He let go of me and grabbed his nose in pain. They never messed with me after that and I began to develop a reputation as a fighter. I also began to develop a strong dislike for white people. Since Roosevelt was predominately white I didn't like Roosevelt at all and I would beg my mother to send me to Garfield. But she wouldn't budge so I stayed at Roosevelt.

I also learned to shoplift during my time at Roosevelt. I hung with a boy in my class named Reggie Laskin. Reggie was another black kid bussed from the south end of Seattle. He lived in the Rainier Vista area. Rainier Vista was Seattle's answer to the projects. They were single story homes grouped together by a maze of little roads that you could only navigate effectively if you were a resident of that area. Rainier Vista, Holly Park, and Yesler Terrace were all communities where low-income families were housed. Most of the tenants were recipients of welfare or in transition from one hardship or another. So Reggie being from this environment was a little advanced when it came to the tricks of survival. There was a 7-11 store around the corner from our school where all of the kids would go to buy stuff at lunchtime. One day I went to the store with Reggie even though neither one of us had any money.

"Marty, you want to go down to 7-11?" Reggie asked right before the lunch bell rang.

"Naw, I don't have any money" I replied.

"Neither do I" Reggie responded, with a sly look in his eye.

"Then why go to the store?" I asked.

"I'll show you how to come-up." Reggie answered.

"Come-up, what's that?" I asked naively.

"Come on I'll show you." Reggie said as the lunch bell rang signaling the start of our 45 minutes for lunch.

Reggie and I walked down to the 7-11 with me eager to find out how to come-up and get candy and snacks with no money. When we got to the store Reggie instructed me to just go over by the video games and hang out until he gave me the signal that it was time to go. When we entered the store there were already a number of kids in there laughing, joking, and purchasing items at the counter. Some kids were in the back of the store playing video games, this being the early 80's when video games that took a quarter were in just about every store you went into. Arcades were also big during this time. After entering the store Reggie and I went our separate ways, him to the candy aisle, and me to the back of the store where the video games were. There were already kids on the three video games so I joined the crowd as if I was watching the game or waiting for my turn. Every once in while I would glance over to see what Reggie was doing. He seemed to be just browsing the aisles as if he were looking for something in particular. After about five minutes of this I heard Reggie yell "Come on man, they don't have it here," he then walked out of the door with me following close behind. Once we were about two blocks from the store Reggie lifted up his shirt and began to pull item after item out of his pants.

"Where'd you get all that?" I asked.

"That's how you come up." Reggie replied. "When the store is crowded and the clerks are distracted you get what you want and tuck it in your pants, just make sure it still looks natural."

I was impressed.

From that day on I would make a stop at the store before school, at lunch time and after school. I didn't try to 'come up' every time I went there but when I had a chance I would take the opportunity to put into practice the skills I learned from Reggie. It actually became easier and easier to pick up items without being detected, so much so that I began to do it at other locations as well.

There was a group of kids in our neighborhood that were a few years younger than I was but they loved to follow me around and do what I did. There was Terrence and Omega who were brothers. Omega was one year older than Terrence and had an odd shaped head, he also was hard of hearing so he had to wear a hearing aid. Because of how he looked we began to call him "Wolf". Then there was Jamal. Jamal was the same age as Terrence, which was about five years younger than I was. Jamal's grandmother owned a lot of property in our neighborhood and she actually had a swimming pool in her backyard. However, as long as I can remember, the swimming pool was always filled with leaves and green mildewed water. I cannot remember anybody ever using that pool. She would also have a lot of late night parties at her house. We began to call it the after-hours and we tried to sneak in every once in a while but we could never get past Jamal's twin aunts. Jamal's older brother Shyhang was in our crew as well. He was a year or two older than Jamal. Next door to me was Porky and Eccee. They were the same age as Terrence and Jamal but they didn't stay in our neighborhood very long.

We would all ride our bikes all over the city getting into all kinds of trouble, but having so much fun. We would stand on the roof of Martin Luther King elementary school and throw rocks and apples at cars passing by then watch and laugh as drivers tried to figure out who did it. We would jump off the roof just for the fun of it. We would jump from portable to portable, a distance of about ten feet, thirteen feet up in the air, but it didn't frighten us back then. It was as if we were fearless and indestructible.

We would fight amongst ourselves but we wouldn't let anyone else mess with anyone in the crew. My brother and I once got into trouble for letting my sister Tash and Omega fight. They were the same age and everything, and it was a fair fight. But family always comes before friendship in my mom's book and we got into trouble for not breaking it up or helping my sister. One time at an open house at a school Terrence attended we all went to enjoy the free cookies, pop, and other treats they always have at school open houses. We were all having a good time running around the school, eating the snacks, and playing basketball in the gym, when Jamal bumped into a little white kid and knocked him down accidentally while chasing the basketball. The kid's dad immediately rushed over and grabbed Jamal by the arm.

"What in the hell do you think you're doing?" He growled.

"It was an accident." Jamal said, becoming a little frightened.

"It was not an accident, I've been watching you little hoodlums run around all night, and I'm sick of it, now look what you've done"

By this time people were beginning to gather as we walked over to assist Jamal. Now Jamal was only nine years old so he was scared and didn't know what to do. But I was fourteen, a freshman in high school and I had begun to develop a strong dislike for white people. So I was not at all afraid, in fact I was upset that he had grabbed Jamal the way he did.

"Let go of him!" I said as we walked up.

"What?"

"I said let go of him, it was an accident."

"It was not an accident; you little bastards have been running around out of control."

"Come here" he demanded turning red with anger.

He then approached me trying to grab me with his right hand while still holding on to Jamal with his left. When he reached for me I ducked and punched him in his right kidney with my left hand. I then caught him under his chin with my right hand with a full uppercut. His head snapped back, his body followed his head and he went backwards falling hard on his back and hitting his head hard on the gym floor.

"Hey!!!" a parent yelled.

"OOOOOOOOOOHHHH!!!" Was my crew's response.

We then took off out of there, laughing and yelling. Not bothering to look back until we were all the way down the block. We ran all the way home not knowing if they were going to come after us or send the police. But we made it home safely and I never heard anything from anyone about the incident. I think Jamal got suspended from school for a couple of days, but he never told the school that it was me who knocked the guy out, and his family was actually glad that I had stood up for him. So everything worked out in the end.

I was actually with the same bunch of guys when I got caught stealing and found out it wasn't as easy or acceptable as I had convinced myself it was. We rode the bus out to the University of Washington to hang out at Arnold's which was the arcade that always had the latest video games. After spending all of our money we decided to go up on the Ave and mess around. Everyone in my crew was now well trained in the "Art of the Come Up" so we were going in and out of stores taking whatever we wanted. For some reason, even though I was a virgin, I decided to take not only candy, but as many condoms as I could fit into my stash spot. We had gone to a number of smaller stores when we decided to go into a Bartell's drug store. After making our rounds I was headed to the door when a large gentleman stepped in front of the entrance. I turned around to look for another exit, but before I could make a move another large gentleman grabbed me by the arm.

"Could you please come with me?" He said. Demanding, more than asking.

By this time the other large gentleman who had blocked the door had joined us and grabbed my other arm. I remember Terrence's eyes as they escorted me to the back of the store. I wish I could say I said something like: "Run, save yourself," but I didn't, I was scared. Terrence and the rest of the crew did run and save themselves though, while I was led back into a little interrogation room in the rear of the store. As we walked in I noticed all of the monitors that were picking up the camera feeds from throughout the store.

"Could you please empty your pockets?" Gentleman #2 asked/demanded.

So I obliged, thinking maybe I can get out of here anyway because I didn't have anything in my pockets. After turning my pockets inside out I began to feel a little smug because all I had was a bus transfer and some half eaten candy from one of the previous stores. Gentleman #1 then walked over to me and attempted to reach into the front of my pants.

"I'll do it," I said, realizing that they were on to me.

I began to pull out my stash of condoms. Between the three stores we had gone to, I ended up with about forty condoms.

"Wow," Gentleman #1 said. "You must be a popular guy".

"You're under arrest" Gentleman #2 stated dryly.

I was then told to have a seat. While Gentleman #1 went to call the Seattle police, Gentleman #2 began to ask me all kinds of questions which I refused to answer. I figured I was already in trouble so I didn't feel the need to talk to this guy who obviously didn't like me and just wanted me out of his store as quickly as possible.

After what seemed like an hour two Seattle police officers arrived, spoke with gentleman #1 briefly, then approached me and asked me to stand, turn around, and place both of my hands behind my back. I was then handcuffed and led out the back of the store and placed into the back seat of a police car. This being the first time I had ever been arrested I was starting to get a little scared.

When we arrived at the precinct I was taken into a booking area where I was fingerprinted while they asked for my phone number, address, age, parent's names, etc... I was then placed in a holding cell by myself. I sat in that holding cell for four hours. When I saw someone approaching the little window in the door I hopped up eager to find out what was going to happen to me. An officer opened the cell door and told me to walk with him down a long corridor. In my mind I was thinking they were about to put me with the rest of the prisoners, and not having any idea what jail was like, but having heard stories, I wondered if I was going to have to fight to protect my manhood. I was then led into a room and told to have a seat. At this point a detective came into the room and told me that I was being released into the custody of my mother and my uncle. I was told that I was not to go back into Bartell's for at least a year, and if I was caught on Bartell's property I would be arrested for trespassing and sent to the juvenile detention center.

I was then taken out and handed over to my mom and my Uncle James. I don't remember what was said in the lecture when we got home but I remember my mom didn't say anything to me all the way home. I had to do a bunch of community service hours and take a theft class twice a week for a month. But the hardest discipline I received was the lectures. After the Lectures I received from my mom and uncle I decided that shop-lifting just wasn't for me. I would go through another theft stage later on in high school when we all got caught up in the smash and dash phenomenon, but for the most part I was never really into stealing from stores after that.

We did steal from other places though. There was a time when we would walk around the neighborhoods that had parking meters and pick the meters. At certain times of day the meters were left open and you were able to lift the lid and turn the handle and get all of the change that was in that particular meter. I went so far as to make a key for the meters in metal shop after I saw someone else make one. This was a good "come up" for a while until too many people got hip to it, then the city changed the meters so they didn't leave them open and our keys didn't work. We would then go around to the parking lots and use a paperclip to pull out the dollar bills that people had put into the slots assigned to their parking spot. This was good for a while until they changed the cash receptacles after getting hit too often. Then there were the times we would walk into 7-11 about five to ten guys deep and grab cases of beer and act like we were taking them to the counter to pay for them then we would all run out of the store and jump into cars and drive off. We would then meet up at someone's house or at the beach and drink beer and smoke weed and laugh about our great escape. But this wasn't until my junior and senior years at Garfield.

For the most part my time at Roosevelt was uneventful except for the race riot and my getting expelled for fighting the junior varsity football team.

When I was a sophomore at Roosevelt somehow a huge fight broke out between the white kids and the black kids. There were about twenty kids from each race fighting in the halls. Then somehow the Mexican kids got involved as well. This was while school was ending for the day so the staff tried to rush everybody out of the school and onto their school buses. This was during forced integration so most of the black students were being bussed in from some other part of town, while Roosevelt was in a white neighborhood in north Seattle. Although I was known for fighting I don't remember taking part in that particular fight. I think that's because our last period teacher rushed us out of the classroom and escorted us straight to the busses. I still remember looking out the window and seeing Mike Rim fighting about five Mexican kids all by himself. Mike was a black dude from my neighborhood. He was three or four years older than I was and he was huge. He played football and he looked like he was on steroids, but I don't think people in my neighborhood knew about steroids back then, so I think he was just big from lifting a lot of weights. Anyway, I remember looking out the window of the bus as Mike threw these kids one by one over this hill, and into the street. He was still tossing them as the bus pulled of so I don't know how the fight ended up, however when we returned to school the next day we found out that about twenty kids had been suspended. There was peace at school for a while, until I fought the football team.

Growing up in Madison valley we would play all kinds of sports. However, my favorite sport was football. I started playing for the Eighty-Niners when I was seven years old even though everybody else on the team was eight and nine years old. I played football every year for the Central Area Youth Association(C.A.Y.A.). I became pretty good. I wasn't the fastest, biggest, or most talented, but I had heart, and I wouldn't back down from a fight, kind of like a Pit-bull. So I was always one of the top ten most athletic on the little league teams I was on while I was growing up. I often wonder now as an adult if I might have gone further in my football career if I would have had a father to teach me some of the fundamentals of the sport, instead of me just coming out and doing the best that I could.

But I digress. In my sophomore year at Roosevelt I went out for the freshman/sophomore football team. As I said, I was pretty good so I made the team. I really didn't think I was given a fair amount of playing time but that might have been because some of the other players had played their freshman year as well so this was their second year on the team. Therefore, the coach was more familiar with their talents. But I didn't see it that way when I was in school. I played tail back and I felt I was just as good as the players who were getting more time than me in that position. For the first few games that didn't bother me that much because I was determined to prove myself. But things changed when we played against Garfield. For one thing I had always wanted to go to Garfield since it was the closest high school to my house and it was predominantly black. Plus my brother, and my sister both went to Garfield and they would always tell me how live it was. But my mom wouldn't let me go there. She insisted I take the bus all the way across town to Roosevelt.

When we got ready to play Garfield I was fired up. This was the game of the year for me. I would be playing against a lot of the kids I played with at C.A.Y.A., so I really wanted to play well. The game started off as any other and it was actually a pretty close game. I wasn't allowed very many carries but when I did I would pick up 5, 8, and sometimes 10-12 yards. So I began to get really angry and discouraged when the coach took me out and put in a kid who had played the previous year, but he wasn't performing as well as I was in this game. When we started losing my anger only grew and grew. I remember pacing the side lines asking the coach to put me back in the game, but for some reason he kept letting this white kid run the ball. When the game was over and we lost I was furious. I shook the hands of the Garfield team then stormed into the locker room. When I saw the dude who the coach put in for me I immediately began to curse him out. I remember being right in his face yelling at him. It wasn't just him I was mad at, I was mad at the system. Being bussed to an all-white school, not being given a fair chance on the field, and then losing to my friends who I would rather be playing with anyway. All of this anger came welling out after that game and I punched that kid so hard I think I broke his nose. Our team was mostly white and I was one of maybe five black kids on the team so when I hit him two or three other white kids jumped on me. Remember this was after the race riot earlier in that year. I remember being in a rage as one kid grabbed me and I hit another kid with my helmet. I was a pretty good wrestler so I broke free from that kid and threw him to the ground. I was starting to kick him when someone grabbed me and threw me into the lockers. I don't remember getting hit but I do remember striking out at every white face that came within two feet of me. I fought and fought until three coaches rushed in and grabbed me. It took three because I had lashed out at the first one in anger when he approached me looking like another white face attacking me.

The next day when I got to school I was called into the office. I was told that I was being expelled from Roosevelt High School. I was surprised and a little shocked. They never asked me why I was fighting. But inside I smiled a little. Because didn't want to be there anyway, and I don't think they really wanted me there either.

After being expelled from Roosevelt I went to Nathan Hale for one semester. I got kicked out of Roosevelt right in the middle of the year so I had to finish a little work at home to make sure I got my grades to transfer. When the second semester of my sophomore year started, I was a new student at Nathan Hale High School. I don't remember much about Nathan Hale other than running track, break dancing, and graffiti. I finished my sophomore year there and then my dreams came true, I transferred to Garfield High School.

Garfield was like the Promised Land to me. Most of my friends from the hood went there, except for Brian who went to O'Dea high school. Shawn and Mark Kilgore went there, Hot Rod went there, and a bunch of cats from C.A.Y.A. went there as well. There were beautiful brown skinned girls everywhere. I was excited even though I really hadn't had many girlfriends up to that point. For some reason most of the girls were into light skinned dudes around this time. I don't know if it was because Debarge was big around that time or what, but a brown skinned brother like me found it kind of hard to pull a sister in those days. All in all, I felt like I had finally arrived.

My brother graduated the year before I got there so when I arrived I was instantly recognized as "Crazy Carl Lawson's" brother. My brother had built up quite the reputation at Garfield. Even though my brother was something of a late bloomer, when he bloomed he burst into the world. When we were younger I was always trying to spend the night over one of my friend's houses. Doobie usually stayed at home. He really wasn't one for spending the night. He was kind of a homebody. He did excel at football and basketball though. He was faster than I was, and even though he was only about an inch or two taller than me in high school, he could easily dunk a basketball with one or both hands. But Doobie was also an artist and he would spend hours drawing pictures. Later in life he would draw a picture of the Tasmanian devil cartoon character holding a shotgun. He then had that picture tattooed on his right arm. I got a tattoo the day after he showed me his. But I got a black panther because I had just read the autobiography of Malcolm X and I was in a militant state of mind. I also considered changing my name to Martin X. I never did though. Later in life when my brother was murdered I remember not really accepting that my brother had been killed, even though I was looking right at him. I didn't believe it was him until they showed me the tattoo of that Tasmanian devil holding a shotgun.

But once again I'm getting ahead of myself.

Everybody at Garfield knew my brother. Through the grapevine I came to find out that in school he was one of the rowdiest, loudest, distracting cats ever. When I got to Garfield I was deluged with stories about how crazy my brother was.

"You're Carl's brother? Dude is nuts." From a cat I met in the hallway.

"Your brother is so crazy." This from some really cute senior girl who said it as if crazy was a good thing.

"He is so crazy"

This seemed odd to me because at home he seemed pretty chill for the most part. He would, however, reveal his crazy side to me in the next couple of years when we started hanging in the same circles.

Since my brother was somewhat of a celebrity at Garfield my transition there was pretty easy. I went out for the football team and although I didn't start on varsity I was second string tail-back. I did start on the junior varsity team. I remember one game where I scored four touchdowns. I quickly made friends with most of the people on the football team, including the white guys. But I was especially close to a group of guys who played football and were in the same grade as I was. We called ourselves the 86ers because we were going to graduate in 1986. All the crews had a nick-name. There were a group of seniors who called themselves "Moo-Sie", kind of a Greek wanna-be crew of senior football players. Then there was 1-5-1 crew. These guys were seniors to but they were more of the hustler type so they took their name from 151 proof rum. Even the girls had crews. The girls in our class had a crew called the "Guess Girls," named after the Guess Clothing line which was big back then.

The 86ers were made up of ten people. L. Rice, Gavin, Terry O'Neal, Chris Scott, Reese Wells, Anton Thompson, Sway Dre, Kush, Joe Carlisle, and myself. We were rough cats. Most high schools had a day called freshman day where the freshman were hazed into high school by getting beat up, or mistreated in some way. We had that as well, but we also had senior day when we, the 86ers, would hunt down and attempt to smash any senior dude we could catch alone or any group of seniors we out-numbered. Even though we were all cool and it was done in good natured fun, you still didn't want to get caught alone. The beatings we administered were no joke. But there was one senior that we didn't mess with even if he was alone and we were three or four deep. That was Slade. Slade played football and he was on the wrestling team. His hands were about twice as big as mine and if he hit you it felt like you got hit with a bag of sand. He was a big solid dude who liked to play around and wrestle until you were bruised or bleeding. So we didn't mess with Slade. Even if you got the best of Slade in a group, there would be a time when you would be alone and Slade would come upon you seeking revenge. None of us wanted to take that chance. We were rough, but we weren't stupid.

I finally started to get some real play from the females when I got to Garfield. I don't know if brown skinned guys were in style then or if I was just riding on the coat tails of my brother's reputation, either way I didn't mind because I was enjoying myself. Up until this time I had kissed a couple of girls, and I had seen a breast or two. Once in the sixth grade when our teacher took our class to California. But mostly from the Playboy books I would sneak and look at when I visited my dad on the weekends. But officially I was still a virgin. I had come close my junior year when I was at home in my room with a beautiful young lady who had recently moved to Seattle from California. This girl was fine. She was a dancer and she had an exotic look that made her stand out in a room full of pretty girls. So we were in my room messing around and even though I was a virgin I had heard a few stories about what love-making was supposed to be like.

"So, what you wanna do?" I asked after about fifteen minutes of kissing and heavy petting.

"I don't know, what do you want to do?" She asked, looking at me with those brown almond shaped eyes.

"You know what I want to do." I said, trying to sound cool even though I was so excited I could almost bust.

"What" she asked in this voice that made me feel as if I was going to bust.

"Well first" I said, "I want to take that shirt off of you so I can kiss you on your neck, then work my way down till you ask me to stop." I replied in a smooth voice, and then I licked my lips like I saw L.L. Cool J do in a video.

"Okay" she said as she stood up and removed her shirt.

I was mesmerized. This girl was beautiful, and she was in my bedroom topless. Well, she still had her bra on but that was just a minor technicality that could be easily dealt with when the time was right. Was this it? I asked myself. Was this finally going to happen? I gently laid her down on the bed then I stood over her and took off my shirt. I was in pretty good shape so the six pack abs caught her eyes for a second. I leaned over her and began slowly and gently kissing her on the neck. Her breathing began to change a little so I figured I was doing okay. Then I moved up to her mouth for a deep sensual kiss. It was going good until I tried a move I had seen on The Young and the Restless. In the soap opera he had gently sucked on her lip while he caressed her body. So I tried that.

"Ow" she said, pulling away abruptly. "Why'd you do that?"

"Do what?" I asked.

"Suck my lip so hard," it's starting to swell up."

"Oh, I'm sorry" I said, embarrassed and starting to wonder if my hopes had been crushed.

"It's okay," she said, "just be gentle."

'Oh Boy,' I thought as I once again began to gently kiss her and softly caress her. 'This really is going to happen'. I was on my way to manhood. I had one hand on her bra clasp in the process of unsnapping it when there was a knock at the door.

"Marty, mom wants you." It was my sister Tash.

"Okay, I'll be there in a minute."

"No, she wants you now." She barked through the door, causing my guest to sit up reach for her shirt.

Needless to say that killed the mood. For her, not for me. But that didn't matter, the moment had passed.

I did finally do the deed later on that year after I started going with a girl named Kenyatta. Kenyatta had transferred to Garfield from Juanita high school in Kirkland. Juanita was a predominately white school where the parents of most of the students were pretty well off financially. So when Kenyatta arrived at Garfield she had an air about her that set her apart from the girls I was used to seeing. I first met Kenyatta one day when a couple of friends and I were in the gym tossing the football around after school. I noticed her and a friend of hers standing over near the gym door watching us. I went out for a pass in their direction and called for the ball. After I caught the ball I continued to run at them and when I got to Kenyatta I gave her the football then picked her up and gently laid her on the ground, as if I had just tackled her. This was my attempt at an ice breaker. She was smiling and giggling so it seemed to be going pretty well until the rest of my crew got involved. When they saw me make the tackle; dedicated football players that they were: they rushed over and dived on my back as I was kneeling over Kenyatta. Before I knew it four guys had jumped on the pile and I was using all of my strength to keep the weight of all of those dudes off of this girl who was lying on her back under me. I just wanted to meet her; I didn't want to crush her.

"Get off me," I yelled good naturedly from my position on my hands and knees. The pile just laughed.

"Seriously, she can't breathe," I said, smiling at Kenyatta.

Concerned for the safety of the young lady the pile began to disperse. Once I was able to stand I helped her to her feet and asked her if she was ok.

"Yes, I'm fine," she said. "Why did you do that?"

"You had the ball." I said, feeling pretty good about my witty reply. "Plus I wanted to meet you, what's your name?"

"Kenyatta," she said smiling.

"How come I've never seen you before?" I asked.

"I just transferred here from Juanita High School in Kirkland."

"Oh," I said. "So what are you about to do Kenyatta, and can I join you?"

"I was just going to my friend's house, but you can walk with us if you want to."

So I did. Kenyatta and I started going together after that. She moved some of her stuff into my locker and we were a happy couple. She met my mom who seemed to like her so she would come over my house sometimes and we would do homework and mess around every once and a while. One day we were in my room and there was no one else home. The messing around started to get a little heavy when she asked me if I wanted to have sex. Oh man, did I ever. We both undressed and got into my bed. After a little more kissing, hugging and caressing, I climbed on top of her to experience what I expected to be one of the greatest moments of my life. I placed myself inside her and the feeling was unexplainable. I had entertained myself quite a few times prior to that but this was beyond comparison. I began to move the way I thought I was supposed to even though I had never made love before. But guys talk and if you listen you're able to pick up a few tips. I seemed to be doing ok for a few minutes until my manhood decided he wanted to do his own thing. I was making every effort to make a good showing on my first time at bat, because she didn't know I was a virgin. But suddenly Mr. Happy didn't want to cooperate with me anymore. It started in my stomach. A very intense feeling of pleasure or euphoria. It then began to make its way down toward Mr. Happy. Before I knew it I was being overcome by this wonderful feeling of orgasmic release. I tried to control it and act as if I was still in the game but I was in over my head. I then tried to play it off.

"Are you done," she asked me when I stopped moving.

"Hold up," I said, hopping up and running over to the window. "I think my mom is here."

We then got up and got dressed. The blood was still rushing to my head so I'm honestly not sure what happened after that. I think I walked her to her car, gave her a kiss and then went back into my room embarrassed about my performance, but reveling in the feeling.

Kenyatta and I stayed together for the rest of that semester. And I did get better at lovemaking. Since she was my first physical love I was sure I had fallen in love with her. Therefore, I was heartbroken when we broke up at the end of the school year. I remember sitting around in my room depressed and playing slow songs for a couple of weeks. Then my brother and I decided to have a party to kick off summer.

The parties that my brother and I threw were legendary. We came up in a time where house parties were the thing to do. For music we drafted a cat named Nathaniel who called himself 'Nasty Nate' when he was D.J.ing. We found out when my mom when was going out of town, then we printed up flyers and distributed them to every high school in the area. Of course most of the people who came were from Garfield, but we did get a lot of people from other schools as well. Mostly girls, the dudes weren't really that welcome, unless they were cool with us and we knew them or someone from their crew. The girls were always welcome no matter where they were from. The more the merrier. After I broke up with Kenyatta I kind of went on a rampage. I was a nice guy, but I really wasn't going to put myself in the position of falling in love again. I began to tighten up my game and getting with girls became easier and easier for me. Our parties were usually jam packed, upstairs and downstairs. We once counted over 300 people in our four bedroom house. We would remove all of the furniture from the living room and that would be the dance floor. We would have the keg or a large tub of spiked punch in the kitchen where partiers could play quarters or take hits from the beer bong. There was room for chilling, drinking, socializing, and smoking weed downstairs in the recreation room. My mom's room and my sister's bedrooms upstairs would be off limits. But downstairs was a different story. Every once and a while one of the homies would ask to use my room or my brother's room to entertain a lady friend. That was only ok for those who were really close to me. Otherwise they would have to go to their car or go home. My lady friends, however, were always welcome in my room. The summer between my junior and senior year I must have had four or five different sex partners. I really wasn't trying to settle down for any extended amount of time so I would let them know this early in the relationship. Usually after we made love a few times, but before I was pressured into becoming part of a couple. All of my relationships ended on good terms though. We always remained friends and sometimes we would hook up again, like Freddie Jackson used to say, "For old times' sake." Life was good.

House parties weren't the only parties we would throw. We would sometimes rent out a hall, pass out flyers and party. These were usually more welcoming to dudes from other schools. We would charge admission to these parties so their money was just as good as the next persons. We also threw parties on the beach. One time we rented a generator and went to a beach where we could light bonfires. We lit a huge bonfire, hooked two turntables and a system up to a generator, fired up a couple of grills and partied. We had a volleyball game going and it was BYOB so everybody was buzzed and having a good time. Until!!!

As I said before my crew was rough so someone had started playing 'Crackem'. The rules to Crackem were that any dude caught slipping was liable to be tackled by any other dude at any time. We tried to set some rules, like no cracking by the fire, no cracking the D.J. or the cook, and no cracking while someone was dancing. These rules held up for a while until people began to get drunker and drunker. An 86er cracking another 86er wasn't a big deal, everyone would laugh and he would get up and try to find someone else to crack. An 86er cracking a non 86er was another story.

I was on the grill cooking when I heard a collective "OOOOOWH!!!"

When I went to see what happened I saw a group of people standing around someone who was lying on the ground in obvious pain.

"What happened," I asked

"L. Rice cracked T." I was told

Now L. Rice was an 86er, one of my closest friends and tough as nails. We would often hang out and people who didn't know us sometimes thought we were brothers. T on the other hand was a pretty boy prep. He was light skinned, handsome, and he always dressed well. He would later in life go on to start three clothing companies and become a multimillionaire. But right now he was lying in the sand in a twisted, moaning, mound of flesh.

"T, are you ok?" A pretty girl asked.

"No," T said, "I can't move."

"Somebody call an ambulance." The pretty girl yelled.

"Yeah," said another girl in the circle.

Now as I said earlier T was a pretty boy prep which meant he wasn't expected to get up after getting hit like he had. Before I knew it he was surrounded by 7 or 8 girls, all concerned for his safety. Someone had called an ambulance and when the ambulance arrived so did the police. So as the EMT's loaded T into the aid car we were questioned about how the accident happened. When the police and the aid car left, that pretty much put an end to the party because all of the girls were now mad at L.Rice for cracking T. We hung out for a little while longer then packed up and left. I did hear that a few cats stayed behind and bet a dude named Dball he wouldn't walk through the hot coals from the bonfire. I think they bet him about $150. He was drunk so he took it. I later heard that he did it and his feet blistered up so bad he had to go to emergency and he couldn't wear shoes or walk for about two weeks. We still laugh about that now.

As I said earlier, I was rarely without a female companion throughout the summer. My bedroom was on the ground level in in the back of the house. So it wasn't unusual for a female friend to be climbing in or out of my window late at night. My sexual prowess had improved considerably since my first attempt so I didn't have a problem finding and keeping willing participants. I still remember most of the girls I was with although a few stand out for different reasons. I went with a couple of light-skinned girls who were actually close friends with one another. They were both very pretty and one would later hook up with my brother. I think women sometimes share the details of their escapades, making their friends curious. I think this is what happened with these two. I got with another girl who I first met at Roosevelt. The first time we got together didn't go as well as I hoped because I had had too much to drink at the kegger where we hooked up. I did however make up for the next time we got together. We made love on a blanket in the Arboretum. I believe it was memorable for both of us. These were really only flings and I didn't really get another real girlfriend until I returned to school for my senior year.

Senior year at Garfield was one of the best, most memorable periods of my life. The 86ers pretty much ran the school. There were dudes on the basketball team who had a bit of stature, but as far as toughness, it was the 86ers. Garfield was known for its sports programs. We won state in track, and basketball in my junior year. We would go on to win state in basketball and track in my senior year as well. In fact I won district in the 300 meter hurdles and went to state in that event and in the triple jump my senior year. I didn't do very well in state though. Partly because we went swimming at the hotel the evening before my event. The reason I won district in the 300 meter hurdles was because Mark Phillips didn't run in that event that day. Mark was fast as lightning. He ran the 100 meter, the 300 meter hurdles, the 100 meter hurdles, and the 4 x 100 meter relay and went to state in all of them. And I think he won state in all of them as well. He also played basketball. His younger brother Peller, who was three years younger than us, was just as talented.

Our football team was very good my senior year, although we sometimes lacked focus. We had talented individuals in every position, and talented individuals backing them up, but at most practices and off the field our heads just were not in the game. In spite of all of that we would have won the Metro title if we had not lost a very controversial game to Blanchet. We scored three touch downs that were all called back because of penalties and we ended up losing 6 to 3. That was the hardest loss of the season. We felt the official took it from us. Blanchet was an all-white school in northern Seattle, and we truly believed that played a part in some of the calls that were made that day.

Aside from that, senior year was live. We had all kinds of rough games we played. One game was the booty game. The object of the booty game was to catch someone unaware in the hallway during lunch or break, sneak up on your victim, jump as high as you could in the air, grab your victims head and smash it against your butt. If you wanted to be extra cruel you would jump up in the air and smash your victims head against the wall with your butt. Since this game was played from the start of the school year to the end of the school year, you had to constantly be on the lookout for participants looking to make you a victim.

Life was good in high school. We were usually in charge of concessions and security at the basketball games so we were always able to make a couple of dollars either at the concession stand or charging people to come in the side entrance. Basketball games were huge at Garfield. Since we were the defending state champions every home game was packed. Not just with Garfield students but with the students from the opposing school as well. They were always hoping that their school would be the one to defeat us. Basketball games were sort of the weekend event in high school. We would watch the game and find out where the parties were after the game was over. The games were also a good place to meet girls from other schools. We had some pretty girls at our school but when you're young the grass is always greener on the other side of the fence. So we were always on the hunt for girls from other areas. It was kind of like a badge of honor to be with a girl that no one knew anything about. I even planned to fly a girl in from California for my prom but something came up at the last minute and she was unable to come. Most of my girlfriends in high school were from other schools. Other than Kenyatta there were three girls that I went out with from Garfield. The first was Mea. Mea was a year younger than I was and she was Jewish. I remember going over her house for dinner and meeting her family. They seemed pretty cool although I really didn't know how they felt about me. I hung out with Mea for a while and we got pretty close but we never had sex because she was a virgin. Then one night we were over one of her friend's house with one of my friends who dated her friend. For some reason she decided that she wanted to make love. It never happened though because I was pretty responsible and I was unable to come up with a condom. She and I soon broke up because I decided that she wasn't really the girl for me. My next Garfield fling was with a girl who liked me for a long time but I wasn't really feeling her at first. She just didn't fit the stereotype for what was attractive back then. She was dark-skinned, and although I was dark-skinned as well I was drawn to light-skinned girls. In spite of that, in time she and I began to spend a lot of time together. She was one of the coolest girls I knew in high school and she was actually a good friend as well as a girlfriend, but you don't really look for those types of values in a woman when you're in high school, so I overlooked her virtue. We ended up hooking up on several occasions and it wasn't until twenty years later that I found out that she was a virgin when we got together. She told me that those are the kind of things a man should know, but I was in high school and far from being a man, even though I was performing mannish acts. My last Garfield fling was a girl named Nicole. Nicole was a white girl. She was the first white girl that I had ever been with. Nicole and I met and had sex on the same day. It was the day after my prom. Since my friend from California was unable to make it to my prom I took Kenyatta. Kenyatta and I got into a small argument in the hotel room after the prom so we didn't consummate the evening as I hoped we would. The next day after Kenyatta left I went over to the room of one of my fellow 86ers and his prom date. He reserved the room another night and his prom dates' friend Nicole was there so we began to talk and pretty soon we were closer then close. We started talking a little after that, mostly just getting together for sex. We definitely weren't dating and we didn't do anything together outside of the bedroom. One time I even played it off and acted like I wasn't with her when Chelsea and her friends drove by while we were at a bus stop. I somehow knew that Nicole was just not the girl for me in the long term, but the sex was good and being with a white girl was certainly different from being with a sister. I remember one time I spent the night at her house. We woke up in the morning and were laying in her bed when her mom walked into the bedroom. Nicole introduced me and her mom began to have a very casual conversation with me about school and other subjects while I lay under the covers naked. I was a bit shocked because I assumed I would be in trouble for being caught in her daughter's bed. It turned out, however, that they had an understanding and it was ok. This was, without a doubt, something I couldn't imagine happening in a sister's house. Nicole and I hooked up throughout the summer before I went to college but then I went to Grambling State University, an all-black college and my views on beauty, manhood, and cultural responsibility began to change. I've never spoke to Nicole again.

College

Attending Grambling State University was one of the highlights of my life. To this day I regret not staying at Grambling for four years and receiving my degree. When I arrived at Grambling in the fall of 1986, there was no one on campus other than a few students and the marching band. Earlier that day I boarded a bus in New Orleans that would take me to Grambling. My brother Doobie and

I flew to New Orleans from Seattle about a week before we were supposed to start school. We stayed with my cousin Denise and her family in New Orleans until it was time to get on the Greyhound and go to school. I headed to Grambling, and my brother headed to Southern in Baton Rouge.

Upon arriving at Grambling the bus dropped me at the bus station, which was also the post office. It was soon apparent to me that there wasn't much else around other than the school campus. Basically, the school was also most of the town of Grambling, Louisiana. I carried my luggage to the admittance office and checked in. I was then given a key and directions to Douglas Hall.

Douglas Hall was one of four men's dorms on the Grambling State University campus. It was situated between the gym and the men's basketball and football dorm. As I approached Douglas Hall I was both excited and apprehensive about how my future at Grambling would turn out. I didn't know of any other people from Seattle who were going to be attending Grambling so I didn't know what to expect from the upcoming school year. But I was excited about my first year of college and I was very much looking forward to my independence. I was in Louisiana, in college, without a parent in sight. What more could an eighteen year old warm blooded young man ask for? Life was good!

I walked into Douglas Hall with my luggage and asked the gentleman in the common area where I could find room 210. He pointed me to a staircase and instructed me that room 210 would be upstairs, second door on the right. As I approached the staircase I took in my surroundings. Douglas Hall was a two story building stretched out in the shape of a straight line. There was a front door on the first floor in the very center of the building that faced the gym. This was the main entrance. Once you entered in you were in a common area with a small office and some couches and chairs situated in an area where guests could come and wait for the student they were visiting to come down from their dorm room. As you enter the building you are facing the common area. If you turn right you can go thru a doorway and enter into the dorm living area. You can also turn left as you enter the building and enter into the dorm area on the other end of the building. The setup was exactly the same on both ends of the building. A staircase that went up to the second floor then a long hallway that stretched to an exit door at the end of a row of doors. There were seven doors on each side of the hall, and each door was a dorm room. On either side there was a community bathroom with three or four urinals and three or four toilet stalls. Towards the back of the bathroom there were seven individual shower stalls. There were five porcelain sinks with mirrors over each one. At the end of the hall near the exit door was another set of stairs that went up to the second floor.

I approached room 210 and opened the door with my key. I walked into the room and looked around. The room was about 14 feet by 14 feet. Directly in front of me was a large window with a table in front of it that stretched the length of the window. To my immediate right as I walked into the room was a sink with a mirror over it. On both sides of the room there were wooden closet areas built into the walls. There were two on each side of the room to accommodate up to four students. There was also a set of bunk beds on each side of the room.

I walked into my dorm room and claimed the bottom bunk on the right side of the room, as I was apparently the first person to arrive. I then decided to go explore the campus.

It was mid-August so I was one of the first students to arrive on campus. I walked around taking in the sites. It was a hot day, yet it was a muggy sort of hot with a lot of humidity in the air. I kicked the red dirt and breathed in the aroma of the South. It felt good to be there as if I were returning home after being away for a long time. As I came around the corner of the auditorium I noticed I wasn't the only student on campus. In the middle of the street in practice formation was the Grambling State University marching band. There were also a number of other young men and women watching as the band members danced and gyrated in unison under the direction of the band leader. This was not the type of marching band I was accustomed to. In Seattle the marching bands walked around playing songs like "Louie, Louie", and "Tequila." This band was playing Cameo's "Word Up" and dancing at the same time. I was very impressed; I had never seen anything like it. I also noticed all of the band members and all of the students watching them were African American. I felt a sudden swell of pride as I realized that I was really a student at Grambling State University. I had set a goal to attend this college and now I was here.

My time at Grambling State University was fun, exciting, and educational. I was getting my first taste of independence and I was thousands of miles away from Seattle. I was the only student from my high school that enrolled at Grambling. There were, however, about eight other Seattle people in the freshman class with me. Other than that I don't think there were any other students from Seattle at Grambling. I was pretty outgoing so I wasn't worried about making new friends or meeting people, plus I knew several of the Seattle freshman from interactions during our high school days. David, Al, Kevin, Bruce, Cedric, and Wendy I knew from Seattle even though we had gone to different high schools. Bruce, Cedric, and Wendy went to Franklin, Al went to Ingram, and I'm not sure what high school David went to. There was also Keith and Tiese. I didn't know either of them before Grambling but we quickly became friends as we began to spend time together and represent ourselves as the Seattle group.

David and Keith were at Grambling to play basketball. They were both pretty good in Seattle and they came to Grambling hoping to play college ball. Bruce, Al, Cedric, Kevin, and I all played football in high school. However, only Kevin had enough nerve to try out for the Grambling football team. He made the team as a walk on and actually got some playing time. To this day I regret not trying out for the team. A number of kids we played against in high school went on to have some pretty successful college careers and a few of them actually played some pro ball. Unfortunately, at eighteen years of age I wasn't the most focused, disciplined, or future sighted individual out there. Bruce, Al, Cedric, and I, we just wanted to have fun. After classes we would hang out in front of the cafeteria and sing Beastie Boy, Run-DMC, or LL Cool J songs. We would get drunk on the weekends and try to get into the fraternity parties. For the most part, we were young and we were enjoying this new and exciting period of our lives. We would also act a little crazy on the weekends after having a few drinks. One time, on the way back to our dorms from the liquor store in the center of the small town of Grambling, we began to mess with Kevin.

Kevin had on some funny looking shorts and Bruce began to talk about how stupid they looked. At one point Al said, "you should just go home and throw those away" and acted like he was trying to yang them off of Kevin. Somehow Al hooked one of the pockets and ripped the shorts on one side. Everyone stopped for a second as Kevin complained, "Man look what you did." The pocket and part of the right leg was hanging off and you could see that a fist sized hole had been torn from the shorts. Bruce, Al, and I just stared and laughed for a second and then Al said, "you might as well just throw them away now," as he grabbed part of the fabric that was hanging and pulled with all of his might. We heard a tearing sound and laughed as Al pulled away half of the fabric from Kevin's shorts. At this point the three of us were laughing and we began tearing pieces of Kevin's shorts off as he cried "stop it, stop it" and attempted to prevent us from grabbing more of his shorts. We continued this for about five minutes and by the time we reached campus we had torn away all of Kevin's shorts and he was pulling his shirt down to cover his underwear. All of us, except for Kevin, were laughing so hard we could barely talk. At this point we decided that we might as well rip off the rest of his clothes and make him run across campus to his dorm butt naked so we began to pull at his shirt and his underwear. Fortunately for Kevin his shirt was made of a better quality material than his shorts and we were unable to rip it. Eventually Kevin was able to elude us and sprint off to his dorm with his underwear in tatters and just some stretching of his shirt where we had been pulling on it. We started to chase him but he was pretty fast and we were all laughing so hard that we could barely run. And so, Kevin escaped as Bruce, Al, and I rolled around on the grass laughing so hard we began to cry. It was another ten minutes before we could get up and go to Kevin's dorm to check on him. When we got there he wouldn't open his door initially but we convinced him that we were not going to mess with him anymore. He eventually let us in and although he was a little mad and extremely embarrassed we were soon all laughing at the hilarity of the situation.

Grambling was also my first real experience with an all-black population. At sporting events I was amazed to see thousands of beautiful African American men, women, boys, and girls getting along and enjoying the game. In Seattle the largest African American event was the black community festival and parade which was usually held in the Central district in July. This was the time when Seattle's African American community would come together and celebrate our culture and community. The festival was larger when I was a child but over the years it became smaller and smaller as most of the African American community was pushed out of the Central Area of Seattle through gentrification. By the time I was a young adult the Black Festival was nothing but a shell of its former self. Even at its prime Seattle's Black Festival was nothing like Grambling. I had never before experienced so many of my people in the same place at the same time. I remember going to my first football game observing 20,000 black people watching the football game. This was a wonderful sight to behold. The music, the energy, the band playing modern hits, this was something that I had not experienced back in Seattle. In Seattle we were used to going to games where there are lots of Caucasians and very few African-Americans in the crowd. We would go to Mariner's, Seahawk , or Husky games but as an African American I was always a very small minority of those in attendance. Here in

Grambling Louisiana, African-Americans were by far the majority. In fact I rarely saw any Caucasians in the crowd, although a few locals would come out to see some of the bigger rivalries. Not only were these games exciting because of the population but they were exciting because of the players, the crowd participation, and the bands. The bands came onto the field doing the latest dances and performing the latest hit songs. The drum-major came out high-stepping, doing flips, splits, and waving his big staff in the air to motivate the band and the crowd to get as excited as possible. There was a female dance group called the Orchesis who would dance while the band played and perform with them at half time. During my first few weeks on campus I actually hooked up with one of the Orchesis members. We only got together one time but we remained friends.

Later on in my first semester at Grambling I did actually have a girlfriend. Her name was Wanda, she was a freshman like me. I'm really not sure how Wanda and I met I just remember that we were kicking it early in the semester before the women's dorms allowed male visitors. We would meet and have dinner together in the cafeteria and then take walks and hang out late into the evening. Wanda was very pretty and her southern accent was fun and interesting to me. I became friends with one of her homeboys who began dating one of my home girls from Seattle. Wanda and I would hang out and go to the dances, movies, or other activities the Grambling Student Union sponsored or we would just pass the time in one another's rooms. Wanda and I had a pretty good run for that first semester but as they say no good thing lasts forever. I decided to break up with Wanda one evening when I woke up from a nap to find her standing over me doing something weird with a playboy magazine open to an article on Satanism. She appeared to be trying to cast some type of spell or conjure some type of incantation and I just wasn't having it. I was already leery of southern women's cooking from my mother who warned me not to eat any women's spaghetti, and so waking up to this really shocked me. I jumped out of bed naked and asked her what she was doing. "Nothing" she replied. "No, you were doing something," I said. I must admit, when I asked her what she was doing my language was not as tame as it is in these pages. This was during the time when Too Short was big and Gangster Rap was taking off so my language was greatly influenced by the music I was listening to. So in all honesty my response may have sounded more like,

"What the f*** are you doing?"

"Nothing," she replied.

"No, you're doing something. Why is this article open and why were you standing over me chanting and waving your hands?"

"Maudy, yur tripping," she replied in that thick southern accent.

"No you're tripping and you need to get the f*** up outta my room." I said, as my anger and surprise continued to grow.

I threw Wanda out of my room half-dressed and sat on my bed looking at the article and wondering what she was trying to do. I talked to Wanda a few times after that trying to find out what she was doing that night but after that incident we were done. Wanda tried to get back with me for a while, even telling me that she was pregnant when I returned from spring break, but she wasn't. Eventually she moved on and began dating a basketball player and she and I were officially over. I still laugh a little when I remember how her new boyfriend would look at me like he had beef.

"Naw G,"I would think, "I don't want any parts of your girl "She's all yours"

I was a little worried about southern girls after that and I didn't date anyone else for the remainder of my time at Grambling. I now know that all southern girls aren't crazy but it took me a while to get over that experience.

All of my roommates at Grambling were cool. For my first semester I bunked with two dudes from Bogalusa, Louisiana. They were funny and I remember hanging out with them and learning about how they grew up. I experienced a lot of firsts with these cats. They would go home on some weekends and bring back different food items. They exposed me to Venison and Boudin which were both pretty good, but I was not brave enough to try the squirrel on a stick they brought back from one of their weekend trips.

I also tried cocaine for the first time with these guys. It was during our homecoming week activities and we were getting ready to go to the concert on campus featuring LL Cool J and Anita Baker. We were all hyped, drinking; smoking weed and acting crazy as we got dressed when one of them asked me if I wanted a snort.

"Sure," I said.

He poured a little powder on the table, chopped it up a little with a playing card and gave me a little straw to snort it with. I had never snorted cocaine so they had to sort of instruct me on what to do and what affects to look for. I must admit, snorting cocaine was not very appealing to me. I wasn't very impressed with the high and I didn't crave another hit. My first experience with cocaine was not very memorable. There was no indication during that time that in less than a year my whole world would change and I would be on my way to becoming strung out and head over heels addicted to crack cocaine. That night we just continued to party and went on to the concert. Later that evening we tied one of my roommates to his bed because he had gotten too drunk and high. He was acting crazy and belligerent so we decided he needed to be restrained for his own safety. He was pretty upset with us and he struggled for a while but eventually he settled down and went to sleep. He slept safely through the night and we untied him in the morning.

My second semester I lived in the basketball dorm with Cedric from Seattle and Fresh, a dude from Flint Michigan. Life was pretty chill during my second semester at Grambling. I wasn't able to go home for spring break so I went Mississippi to stay with my grandmother. Cedric went with me and we met my brother Doobie there. My uncles were pretty excited to see us and they took us up to Jackson State for a basketball game. Unfortunately, we drank too much in preparation for the game and never made it in. Cedric ended up getting sick so we turned around and headed home. After spring break we returned to Grambling to finish out our first year of college. I spent a lot of time hanging out with a group of football players from Atlanta and my Seattle crew.

I finished my first year at Grambling on the Dean's list. I hadn't fully committed to the school so I just sort of coasted through. I decided that the campus was too rural and I didn't want to return. To this day I regret not going back. The instructors were good and one of my favorite classes was an English composition course I took. But I was young and immature so I decided I wanted to transfer to Morehouse. I didn't know what the transfer process was so I just didn't reregister at Grambling and I didn't apply to Morehouse in time to be accepted for the upcoming school year. I'm not sure what my parents were thinking during this time but I wish they had helped me better navigate this transition.

In May of 1987 I returned to Seattle. I got off the plane and my mom picked me up from the airport and brought me home. I grabbed a baseball bat and stood on my porch looking out over the neighborhood that I hadn't seen in almost a year. I decided to take a walk and see what the boys in the hood were up to. As I was walking down the street a yellow Volvo pulled up and my brother Doobie hopped out before the car came to a complete stop. He returned from Southern a few days before me and he was already in the mix. He was happy to see me.

"Marty, what's up?" he said.

"Nothing, just chillin," I replied, "What are you guys doing?"

"I came to see you" he said.

Doobie was very excited to see me. He and I were very close and we did most things together. There were a few girls in the car he had just jumped out of and he introduced me to the driver. Her name was Meko.

"Hi Meko," I said, "It's nice to meet you."

"It's nice to meet you as well," she said, "your brother has been talking about you all day, 'my brother's coming home, my brother's coming home' is all he has been saying."

73

"Well I am glad to be home" I said as Doobie turned the music up and began singing some song on the radio.

I was glad to be home and I was glad to be with my brother. We made some small talk and I learned that Meko was born and raised in Seattle; she was my age and lived in the south end. Meko was pretty and nice but I had no idea on that day that she would one day become my wife. Eventually Meko and her friends left and Doobie and I continued our tour of the neighborhood. It was good to be home. Within months my whole world would be upended but for now I was home and happy.

Chapter 3

INTO THE DARKNESS

My son, do not despise the chastening of the LORD,
nor be discouraged when you are rebuked by
Him; For whom the LORD loves He chastens, and
scourges every son whom He receives.
Hebrews 12:5-6

Prelude to a Journey

Much had changed when I returned to Seattle. During my youth and high school days I'd gotten into a lot of fist fights. My brother Doobie and I were pretty well known for fighting and winning. We also had a crew of cats who were ready and willing to fight whenever the opportunity presented itself. I had gone to jail several times for fighting and I had a few misdemeanor charges of assault as a result of these altercations. This was in the days of fair fights when two people went toe to toe and the stronger combatant prevailed. I relished these moments and although I didn't instigate many fights I wouldn't back down from a challenge either. So occasionally a fight would find me when I was in no way looking for trouble.

One night I was driving my mom's car and hanging out with Doobie, DoRight, and a female friend named Melanie. It was Friday night so we decided to go to Dick's on Broadway to see what was happening. Dick's is the same hangout spot that Sir Mixalot sang about in his Posse on Broadway song. When we got there it was packed. As we drove down the alley behind Dick's looking for parking we pulled up alongside another car heading in the opposite direction. For about a minute or two we were right next to this car as we both waited for traffic to clear out in front of us. I didn't know this at the time but at some point my brother Doobie, who was in the front passenger seat, did or said something to offend the dudes in the car next to us. I was totally oblivious to his actions and pulled forward when the path cleared a little bit. I was able to move about three car lengths forward and make a left into a parking lot when suddenly there was someone at my window throwing punches at me through the open window. Surprised I put the car in park and leaned away from the door while at the same time trying to open the door so that I could get out of the car. Unfortunately the guy who was swinging at me had his hand on the knob used to unlock the door so I was unable to open the door until I got his hand off the door. When I was finally able to open the door I got out of the car and began to thoroughly kick this dude's a**. While I was fighting my brother was beating up two guys and DoRight got out after me and began to help my brother.

We mopped these guys up pretty easily and they ended up limping back to their car and driving away. We continued to hang out at Dick's for a while until I noticed a police officer across the street in the Jack in the Box parking lot looking at us while one of the dudes we fought earlier pointed and gestured in our direction. I got Doobie's and DoRight's attention and we walked across the street to see what the dude was telling the police officer about us. As we approached them the woman officer who was talking to the dude told us to stay where we were while her partner approached us. The officer approaching us didn't ask us any questions he just immediately told me to put my hands behind my back.

"For what'" I said.

"Just do it," he responded.

"For what," I asked again, "They started it."

The officer still insisted that I put my hands behind my back so that I could be handcuffed. I refused and folded my hands across my chest in front of me. The officer, who was a large white man, began to try to pull my arms apart while his partner approached to assist him. By this time my brother and DoRight had moved off to the side and were watching what was going on. Before I knew it the female officer had called for backup and there were six officers on me trying to pull my arms apart. I was pretty strong as I had just returned from college where I lifted weights often and ate well so I was in the best shape that I had been in my life. So basically, the officers were unable to pull my arms apart. They threw me up against the police car and tried to pry my arms apart with their Billy clubs, all while yelling for me to release my arms and place them behind my back. I heard my brother yelling for me to let go of my arms as I was thrown on the ground. I rolled on my stomach with my arms crossed under me and they began to put their knees on my back and head trying to get leverage to pull my arms apart. This went on for a few minutes or so until I heard a car pull up and a barking dog. Next I felt a police dog biting my right foot. I yelled out in pain and said "ok" as I released my arms. They pulled the dog off of me and cuffed my hands behind my back. They then zip tied my feet together and hog tied me by connecting my handcuffs to the zip tie on my feet. I was then placed in the back seat of the patrol car on my stomach. They transported me to the East precinct and transferred me to a holding cell where I was left hog tied for about an hour before someone came to take the restraints off of me. A while after this the officer who was in charge of the dog came in to look at the wound from the dog bite. I was booked and processed and then transferred to the King county jail where I stayed a couple of days until I was released on bail. I was charged with assault on the dudes we fought and obstruction of justice for refusing to submit during an arrest attempt. I took the case all the way to trail and was found not guilty on all counts. I could have even sued the city for the police dog bite but I only had a public defender and he wouldn't advise me of my rights to pursue compensation for the police negligence.

But like I said, when I returned to Seattle after my first year in college nothing was the same. During the mid-80's Blood and Crip gang members began moving up to Seattle from California. By 1986, my senior year in high school, the gangs from California had begun to take hold in the Central District and south end of Seattle. When these gang members came they brought crack cocaine and guns. Whereas we were used to fighting head up from the shoulders, these cats would shoot first and ask questions later. There were a few Seattle dudes who hooked up with these crews early on so there were a few Bloods in the Valley but most of my crew didn't join up with these gangs. Quickly they spread through Seattle promising money and violent prestige to all who joined their ranks. In the Central District the Bloods set up shop in some parts of the Valley and East Union street while the Crips claimed Cherry Street and areas in the south end. I didn't have many run ins with these gangs early on but other Seattle cats were fighting with them as they tried to claim territory in the neighborhoods where Seattle crews called home. Eventually some Seattle dudes with family connections to Chicago organized the Seattleites and created various Folk Nation chapters in Seattle. These groups quickly established Gangster Disciple and Black Gangster Disciple families to prevent the continued spread of the Crip and Blood influence in Seattle. Shooting took the place of fighting and drug dealing took the place of partying and break dancing.

Upon my return to Seattle, I was thrust into a culture where money was power. Kenyatta was a year younger than me so we reconnected after she asked me to take her to her high school prom. After the prom she and I became a bit of an item and we were together almost every day. At some point Kenyatta and her cousin gave me $50 to buy my first quarter of marijuana. Soon I was selling grams and quarters of weed and enjoying a limited amount of financial prosperity. I did this for a month or so until DoRight and I were in a weed house and a dude DoRight knew from California came in and introduced us to crack cocaine.

"What are you guys working with?" He asked us.

"We got the tret" DoRight said, the tret meaning we had the treacherous weed.

"Is that all you're working with?" he asked.

"Yeah, what are you working with?" DoRight asked.

"I got that white," he said. "You make more money faster with the white."

He then showed us a little cookie of cooked up cocaine which he said was a half-ounce. He said he would cut it up and sell $20 dollar pieces and he would make about $1500 off of a $400 investment. This sounded really good to me and DoRight as we were only selling $10 grams of weed and making about $20 profit from each quarter and $80-$100 profit from each ounce of weed. The California cat told us he would give us double up which means that if we spent $50 dollars he would give us $100 worth of crack cocaine. This was very appealing as it meant we could double our investment quicker and with less of an investment. I gave him $100 and he gave me 12 $20 rocks which would net me $240 when sold. DoRight did the same and with that, we were in the drug game.

I had never really been exposed to crack cocaine so I was surprised by its appeal. During my senior year of high school there were a few of my friends who were smoking crack but I never saw them do it and I only heard rumors about them. I had also kicked it with a few cats that had nice cars and money but I was completely naïve to how they were getting their money. This was until I got into the drug game and began to learn who was balling and who was slanging weight.

DoRight and I soon found some spots in the neighborhood where people would come looking for crack. We called them fiends or crack heads and we were awed by how desperate some of them acted to get what we had to offer. We learned that crack was in high demand and we could sell out in a couple of hours while sitting around smoking weed and drinking beer. When we would sell out we would page DoRight's partner from California and he would call us back and then come meet us so we could re-up. After the third or fourth re-up he told us that we could make more money and worry less about the police if we found a house to work out of. This made a lot of sense and so the next time DoRight and I were on the block we began to inquire among our customers to find out if any of them had a house that they would be willing to let us work out of. Eventually an older woman who we called Auntie invited us to her house and said we could sell out of there if we gave her a $20 rock every hour. We agreed and we went to her house where we paid her for the first hour. Auntie went into the back room with her roommate to smoke and DoRight and I sat at the kitchen table to roll up a joint. We sat there for about 30 minutes with no one coming through when suddenly there was a knock at the door. I got up to answer the door thinking we had our first customer in our new spot.

"What's up? What you need?" I asked when I opened the door and saw a middle aged woman with a skinny dude behind her.

"What do I need? Nigga what do you need? She asked as she pushed passed me. "Where's Grace?"

Grace was Auntie's roommate.

"They're in the back room," I said as I sat back down at the kitchen table.

She made her way to the back of the house while the skinny dude stood by the door looking at DoRight and I. Suddenly the dude pulled out a chrome 357 magnum and headed towards us. My heart began to pump rapidly as I wondered what this guy was going to do. He walked over to the table, pulled up a chair, sat down, and placed the gun on the table facing us.

"What are you guys doing?" He asked.

"Auntie said we could work out of here" I said.

"Didn't you know this is Mr. Tate's house?" He asked us.

"Naw," we said, "we've only been here about half an hour."

"Well," he said, "you guys have to leave now; we have to talk with Grace and Auntie."

He then stood up and went over and held the door open so we could leave. DoRight and I quickly exited the house and went across the street to see what was going to happen. The house was on 23rd street right across the street from a barber shop where one of our friends worked so we went over there to watch the house and wait. After about 30 minutes Auntie came out of the house. She stood on the porch and looked up and down the street. Soon she spotted us and motioned for us to come back over to the house.

"What do you want to do?" I asked.

"Let's go see what they want," DoRight said.

So with some reservation we went back to the house and found Grace sitting on the couch with the lady visitor sitting at the table and the skinny dude standing in the kitchen. When we walked into the house Auntie introduced the woman as Mama and the skinny dude as Eyes. Eyes was called this because he was a black dude with green eyes. Mama asked us to sit at the table so they could talk to us. We soon found out that this was a house that Mr. Tate's people worked out of and no one else was supposed to be doing any business out of it. Auntie had gotten impatient while waiting for Mama and Eyes to return and she had gone out to cop something on her own. That's when she found us. Mama and Eyes weren't upset with us in fact they wanted to know if we wanted to work with them. They told us that all we had to do was sit in the house and make sales and we would be paid from each pack we moved. They said we could start today by sitting here and selling until the pack was gone and we would be paid about $100 a pack. A pack was a quarter ounce which was about $700 worth of cooked up cocaine. They said that after we were done with each pack all we had to do was page them and they would come and collect the money and bring us more dope. DoRight and I decided that this was a pretty good deal as we would be paid for just sitting and moving product and we didn't have to invest our own money. So we told them that we would do it. Then came the warning. We were told not to F*** with Mr. Tate's money or there would be serious consequences. Eyes said he didn't want to have to come looking for us to collect and if we were placed in a house then that is where we should be until the pack was gone. We quickly agreed as we had no intentions of trying to get over on these guys. We actually thought it was a good deal. Mama then told us the house rules, gave each of us a quarter ounce of chopped up rock, and we began our employment with Mr. Tate.

That first night we saw that moving rock from this house was in fact way faster and easier than standing on the corner. The customers came to the house in greater numbers because it was safer to do business and they knew that the product was good. They didn't have to worry about getting burned by some kid who sold them fake dope or ran off with their money. So from early evening until around 2am we had a steady stream of customers every fifteen or twenty minutes. Most came for a $20 rock. We often saw these customers several times that night because they would buy their rock and then leave only to come back in an hour or so to buy another $20 rock. They would do this throughout the night until their money was gone and then they might show up asking for a $10 rock. We didn't sell $10 rocks so we would have them put in with someone else and let them work out the details of how to share it among themselves. After purchasing their product the customers were then escorted out the house so that they knew they were not welcome to smoke on the premises. There were those customers who came looking to spend more money and if they needed a place to sit and smoke Grace and Auntie would let them sit in one of their back rooms and smoke if they paid the house ladies, Grace and Auntie, a $20 rock per hour. Grace and Auntie actually did really well in these situations because they would collect payment and then sit in the room with the customer and help them smoke their product. If the customer had any money left after their initial purchase Grace or Auntie would get the money and come get more product from us and return to the room where they would resume smoking until the customer was all out of money. The customer would then be shown the door and told he or she was welcome to come back when they acquired more cash. Throughout the night DoRight and I would smoke weed, drink beer, and watch TV, occasionally opening the door for customers until our packs were sold. We also sold our own personal packs by alternating rocks from our own supply with the rocks that we got from Mama. By 1am we were out having sold almost 3 quarter ounces of rock or $2100 worth of crack in about 8 hours. We paged Mama who soon called us back and told us that she would be through later with more product.

While we waited DoRight and I just chilled watching TV and talking about different customers we had dealt with that night. Grace and Auntie on the other hand were quite high and very agitated at the realization that there was no more dope in the house. They smoked up the payments from Mama and the payments they received from the customers and they were impatient for another hit. We called this fiending as crack heads were referred to as fiends so when they wanted more and were acting erratic they were considered to be fiending.

During this time of fiending our hosts walked around a lot looking on the floor for pieces of rock that might have dropped. They would occasionally pick up something and taste it to see if it was a rock. They smoked cigarettes back to back and asked DoRight and I for some of our beer, only to quickly drink it and ask for more. After about a half hour of this I gave Auntie $10 and sent her to the store to buy her some cigarettes and a few more

40 ounce bottles of Old English, our drink of choice. Grace was a little more composed than Auntie. She asked us if we were hungry, to which we both responded "yes." She then began to fry some chicken that had been thawing in the refrigerator. It wasn't until this point that I realized that neither Auntie nor Grace had eaten anything the whole time we were there. DoRight and I snacked on chips, cookies, and other junk foods we found in the kitchen but no one else had eaten anything.

When Auntie returned with the beer and cigarettes the chicken was almost done. Grace and Auntie sat at the kitchen table drinking from the 40 ounce I gave them and smoking Newport cigarettes. Since this was the first day we met them they soon began to make small talk and ask us questions about ourselves. They were quite surprised to find out that we didn't smoke crack. Later on I would find out that most of the people who dealt in the crack business were smoking, or had smoked crack at some point. Even later in life I would learn that if they had not smoked and remained in the business they would begin smoking at some point. I learned this lesson both from observation and from my own personal period of crack addiction which would envelop me less than a year after my introduction to crack cocaine.

Finally the chicken was ready and Grace brought DoRight and I a plate which we quickly devoured. The chicken was very good and it was clear to me that Grace was a different person when she wasn't smoking crack. I'd just met her but I respected her as I would any older African American woman. We thanked her for the meal and resumed watching TV while we waited for Mama's return. Occasionally there would be a knock at the door as a customer came seeking to make a purchase but after telling four or five people that we were waiting to re-up we just stopped answering the door.

Mama didn't get back until around 8am. DoRight and I nodded off but when we woke up we found that Auntie had been up all night. Grace went to bed around 3am but Auntie stayed at the kitchen table drinking beer, smoking cigarettes, and eagerly awaiting Mama's return. Around 8am I was wrenched out of my sleep on the sofa by a loud knock on the door. Auntie immediately ran to open the door and I could almost feel her joy and relief when she realized it was Mama.

Mama walked in, said "Good Morning," and sat at the kitchen table. But this time her companion was not Eyes. Instead she was accompanied by a large, scruffy looking white man. Mama introduced him as Dan, and we would later find out that Dan, like Eyes, was an enforcer for Mr. Tate. They were both always packing heat and were ready, willing, and eager to violently confront anyone who interfered with Mr. Tate's business.

Dan went into the back room with Grace and Auntie while Doright and I handled our business with Mama. We separated our personal pack money from the money we owed from Mr. Tate's packs earlier so we each handed over $700 to Mama. She counted the money quickly and gave each of us $100 dollars for the night's work. I was feeling pretty good. I made over $400 in one night while drinking beer, smoking weed, and watching TV. This seemed like the business to be in.

Mama told us that Mr. Tate wanted us to work out of this house for a while and if we could keep doing what we'd done on our first night that he might move us to some houses that made even more money. She also said that business was slower during the day and too much daytime traffic made the house hot so they didn't want us slanging from the house before 6pm. This made sense. So we agreed to come back later that evening to open up shop. Mama gave each of us anther quarter ounce and DoRight and I left with the understanding that we would return around 6pm. DoRight and I decided that although we were getting packs from Mama it was still a good idea to have our own packs to supplement our income otherwise we would only be making $100 a night when making $400 a night doing the same thing felt so much better.

DoRight and I worked out of this house for a couple of weeks and we were doing really well financially. So good in fact, that my brother Doobie, a friend named Fred, and my homie Greg wanted to get in with us. After talking to Mama we were all introduced to Mr. Tate. Mr. Tate was a middle aged African American man from California. We soon found out that Mr. Tate had houses like Grace and Auntie's all over Seattle. Since there were five of us he put us in some apartments he had in the south end in a low income apartment complex off of Martin Luther King and Kenyon.

Mr. Tate controlled two apartments in this apartment complex so two of us posted up in one apartment and three of us posted up in the apartment on the other end of the complex. There were more people in this complex so we found out that there was a lot more traffic coming through. We were also able to continue selling in the daytime because of the demand and the isolation of the apartment entrances. In these apartments each one of us was able to go through two packs in 8 to 12 hours. On the first three days of the month we were going through two to three times as much product. When we ran out Mama would bring us more product or we would walk to Mr. Tate's house to give him the money we made, get paid, and re-up.

After a couple of weeks of this we were sitting around getting high and we began to calculate how much money we were making for Mr. Tate. We figured that we were selling about an ounce and a half of rock a night on regular days and twice that on the first few days of the month. This equaled about $2,500-$3,500 a night on average and about $12,500-$17,500 a week when we worked Tuesday night through to early Sunday morning. Out of this gross he was only paying each of us $150 -$200 a night which equaled about $3,750-$5,000 a week. This meant that after paying us and copping ounces at $800 a piece he was making about $4,000-$6,000 profit a week from our two apartments alone. Plus we figured that with the amount of work we were moving he was probably getting product in bulk and only paying about $400 to $500 per ounce if he was buying quarter kilos and even less than that if he was buying kilos. This meant that he was making about $8,000-$12,000 off of the two spots we worked. After doing these calculations we decided to quit working out of Mr. Tate's houses and set up our own spots.

Since most of us were from the valley we decided that we would look to establish some spots in our neighborhood. We didn't have as much foot traffic as the apartment complex but there was enough demand in our hood for us to set up numerous houses to work out of. Unfortunately we weren't as organized as Mr. Tate so we each broke off and began to do our own thing. I began to hang with my brother and my 86 homie Sway from Garfield. We would sit in spots and drink, get high, and rank on one another for hours and take turns making sales that were coming through. Some of the homies went on to work with some serious weight and became considerable ballers in a sense. I never really aspired to be the biggest dope dealer on the block so I was content with moving a couple ounces a week and having enough money to stay high, drunk, buy the latest Jordan's, a few outfits, and floss with a few females.

At some point I established my own houses that I worked out of. I'd go in and sit around watching TV while runners brought customers to the house. I paid the runners a $20 rock for every $100 worth of sales they brought me and I paid the house a $20 rock for every hour I sat and sold from the premises. I ran a couple of spots that I would sell out of in the valley and a couple of spots at the tip of the valley near 20th and Madison and 21st and John. At a couple of these houses I trusted the owners of the house enough to leave packs with them for them to sell. I would drop off a $100 or $200 pack and come back through when they paged me to indicate that they needed more work. One night while I was in my spot on 21st and John for some reason I decided that I wanted to try crack cocaine. I was sitting and talking with the houseman when I asked him how to take a hit. I gave him a piece of a $20 rock and he placed it on his glass pipe and took a slow pull. I watched as the white smoke filled the pipe and he slowly inhaled.

After three or four seconds of inhaling he removed the pipe from his mouth and slowly blew the smoke from his nose while holding one nostril. After he had expelled all of the smoke his behavior changed. Whereas before he was quiet and subdued after the hit he was instantly talkative and animated. I wanted to know what this feeling was. Today I realize that this was one of the most critical points of my life but on that day I didn't know that the decision to try crack would totally change and almost destroy my life.

He handed me his pipe and I asked him how big a piece I should put on. I broke off half of what remained from the $20 rock I used to give him a hit and I placed it in the pipe and lit the end with the lighter.

"Don't pull like you're smoking weed," he said, "pull slow."

I pulled slow and watched as the white smoke filled the pipe. I continued to inhale for a few seconds and then I held my breath like I did when I smoked weed.

"Now blow it out your nose," he instructed.

I blew the smoke out of my nose and was instantly overcome by the most powerful high I had ever experienced. It seemed as if all of my senses were heightened. I could hear better, see better, and I thought my mind had become enlightened in some way. My heart beat began to increase and I stood up.

"Whoa," I said

I had never experienced anything like what I was experiencing after that first hit and words fail me as I look back and try to describe what I felt. What I do know is that I liked it.

"You got a major," he said, indicating that I had gotten a major or large hit.

I couldn't speak at the time but in my mind I was in complete agreement. The high was intense and I instantly understood why this drug was in such high demand.

I started smoking crack in November of 1987. Initially my life wasn't impacted greatly by this development. I would still make money and occasionally I would go to one of my houses and take a couple of hits while chilling in the house making sales. I never let my customers know I took the occasional hit and I had to stop fronting packs to the house man who I smoked with because he came up short a couple of times after he saw me smoke and I realized that him seeing me smoke gave him the impression that I was soft in some way. I didn't get physical with him for coming up short but I did let him know that he would have some serious problems if he thought my puffing gave him the right to f*** with my money. After that I didn't puff in any of the houses I sold out of. I would go by a spot where I knew a cool couple lived and I would hit a few rocks with them before heading down to the neighborhood bar to meet up with my crew. I would meet up with my crew, drink rum and coke, and plan our activities for the evening. Nobody knew I was smoking or if they did we never talked about it. Everything pretty much continued to operate as usual.

In December of that year I found out that K was pregnant. Doobie, DoRight, and I decided that we were going to save our money and move to Atlanta on January 1st 1988 so I was working on making as much money as I could before that date. My mom lost our house in the valley and moved to an apartment in Tukwila. She never told us she was having trouble making the mortgage payments and if she had I'm sure my siblings and I could have helped her out. Later in life I began to think that maybe she was tired of taking care of us through all of or mess and she needed to get out of the valley in order to get a break. After my mom moved out I stayed in the house with my brother and sister until the power was cut off. We used it as a party house and we would even sell a little work out of there. Eventually the neighbors called the police and complained that we were operating a crack house but by that time we were ready to leave. I regret not being more of a man and helping my mom keep her house. When I drive through the neighborhood now, the once all black neighborhood has been transformed into a upper middle class predominately white neighborhood with the house I grew up in costing upwards of $500,000.

I now recognize the same type of gentrification happening in other historically black neighborhoods in cities across the nation but at the time when I could have made a difference in my neighborhood I was too ignorant to do the right thing.

When January came my brother changed his mind. For some reason he decided he wasn't going to move to Atlanta. DoRight and I decided we were still going and we made plans to leave on January 3rd. While I was at Grambling Kenyatta was in a car accident that injured her right leg pretty badly and she was waiting for a settlement from the insurance company. She told me that when she got her settlement she was going to give me $5000 for the move so I was hoping she got it before we left. On January 3rd my mom took DoRight and I to the Greyhound bus station downtown and we purchased one way tickets to Atlanta, Georgia. K met me at the bus station and while we were waiting for the bus we snuck into the bathroom and had sex in one of the stalls. After we were done K gave me $1000 and said she couldn't give me the whole $5000 because she didn't get as much from her settlement as she had hoped. We had to run a little because one of the custodians saw us coming out of the bathroom together and said he was going to go get security. So I quickly kissed K, hugged my mom, and DoRight and I boarded the bus to Atlanta. I had a couple of suitcases, $1000 from K, $1000 from my dad, and a few thousand dollars from slanging and I was on my way to Atlanta.

The bus ride to Atlanta was pretty uneventful and definitely not a ride that I would say I enjoyed. We did, however, have plenty of weed and we were very excited about what awaited us in Atlanta. So those two elements helped the time go by faster. After 3 days on the Greyhound bus we pulled into the Atlanta bus station. We hadn't really developed a plan of action for after we arrived in Atlanta, we just decided where we wanted to go and boarded the first bus headed in that direction.

"What do you want to do?" I asked DoRight.

"S*** I don't know," he responded. "We probably need to get us a room first."

"I'm down with that," I said. "Let's get one over by Morehouse and Spelman."

We knew that Morehouse was across the street from Spelman but before our arrival we didn't know about all the other Historically Black Colleges and Universities that were located in the same vicinity as Morehouse and Spelman. We hopped into a taxi and asked the driver to take us to a reasonably priced hotel near the colleges. The driver began to drive and we took in sights as we traveled through the city. I had just finished reading the Autobiography of Malcolm X again and I was a big fan of Public Enemy and KRS ONE so I was overjoyed at the thought of being around so many college aged African American men and women. We heard that Atlanta was live and that it was the place to be for young black people. We were both eager to experience something very different from the predominantly Caucasian environments that we were accustomed to experiencing in Seattle. I even considered changing my name to Martin X again before deciding against it. We were young, black, free, and with 10 to 15 thousand dollars between us we figured we had enough money to do whatever we wanted to do.

We rented a room for two weeks, set our bags down, and went out to explore the city. The area around the campuses was pretty quiet because all of the students were on winter break but there was still a lot to do in the area with all of the local people that lived there. We quickly found a strip mall area near the schools and sat down to eat at a Popeye's fried chicken restaurant. They didn't have Popeye's in Seattle so this alone was an adventure. After eating we walked to the MARTA and took the train to Lenox mall. We walked around the mall for a while looking at all of the beautiful black women and trying to talk to a few of them to find out what was going on in the town. We weren't able to find anything to get into so we headed back to the room. Over the next several days we were able to find a bunch of parties and events to keep us occupied. We stayed in the room we rented for two weeks and then we moved into another room that was closer to the campus complex. The students returned from break and there was a lot of activity on and around the campuses. Before we knew it, DoRight and I had been in Atlanta for a month just partying and kicking it. We decided we wanted to stay and if that was going to happen then we needed to get an apartment and jobs.

Finding an apartment wasn't as difficult as I initially thought it would be. I used my parents as references and we had cash to cover first, last, and the deposit. I think we actually paid for three or four months in advance on a one year lease. The apartment we rented was in downtown Atlanta right across the street from the Fox Theater. It was a one bedroom apartment on the 8th floor of the building. There was a grocery store and a restaurant on the ground floor of the building and fast food joints up and down the blocks around us. There was also a MARTA station about a block away and a Kroger food store within walking distance. We figured that we were in a pretty good spot. We rented a couch, a bedroom set that included a queen sized bed, a nightstand, a dresser with a mirror, and a five drawer chest, and we also rented an additional queen sized bed. DoRight and I flipped a coin to decide who would get the bedroom and DoRight won. He set up the dresser and mirror, nightstand, and one bed in the bedroom and I set up the couch, the chest, and the other bed in the living room. I put up some posters of Public Enemy, Appalonia, Eric B and Rakim and a poster from the Less Than Zero soundtrack and I was good to go.

The first night there we were looking for something to get into and while looking out of our living room window I noticed a strip club across the street from our apartment building. Being healthy heterosexual young men this piqued both my and DoRight's interest. So we headed down to check it out. When we got there we found that it wasn't so much a strip club as a bar where there was an occasional woman who would dance on the bar topless. There were also a few cute servers who walked around in sexy outfits serving drinks and flirting with the customers but it definitely wasn't what we expected. In spite of our disappointment we hung around for a while drinking and talking with one of the servers as we tried to get an idea about how to make some moves in Atlanta. We would later find real strip clubs like Magic City and The Blue Flame but for now this place would do.

We now had a furnished apartment, and just in time as both of our dollars began to run low. We didn't know anything about the city so we had no intentions of trying to hustle out here, we needed jobs. DoRight found a job before I did. He got hired at some restaurant a few blocks from our apartment. After submitting applications for about a week I eventually got hired at a Wendy's restaurant across the street from our apartment. I never worked fast food before and I didn't look forward to minimum wage but I needed an income immediately. It was the first or second week in February and I had only been on the job two days when my homie Sway called to say they were about to board a plane in Seattle and he was coming to Atlanta. Sway was a baller. He had been in the game for much longer than I had and he was much more driven towards amassing large sums of money from the dope game. On the day I found out Sway was coming down I also learned that Meko was coming down to visit one of her best friends who was attending Spelman. My brother Doobie took Meko to the airport on the very same day Sway left so somehow Meko met up with Sway at the Atlanta airport. Sway came with another friend of ours named Beard. After meeting up at the Atlanta airport Sway, Beard, and Meko planned on getting a rental car to come to our apartment. Unfortunately they were unable to rent a car at the airport because none of them had a credit card. And in spite of the large sums of money Sway offered to the rental agents he could not convince them to rent the group a car. Finally, we called my cousin Melanie who was also a student at Spelman and she went out to pick them up from the airport and bring them to our apartment where DoRight and I were waiting.

It was good to see our friends. Meko and I were more familiar having talked a little since our first meeting months ago. One time I surprised her by picking her up at a house party we were throwing. As she walked down the stairs I leaned over the railing, grabbed her under her arms, and lifted her up to the top of the stairs. She was a little surprised and freaked out so she ran out of the house and waited outside for her ride. Since that night we'd spoken again and become friends.

Sway was now what I considered gangster. He was always looking for a way to make money and he was quick to shoot at anyone who crossed him. He had been one of the first Seattle cats to hook up with the Bloods from California so he was deep in the gangster lifestyle. Beard was a homie who everyone liked to kick it with. Beard was funny as hell. He could rank on you until you wanted to fight or joke and act in a way that made any situation more fun. When they arrived Sway gave me a couple hundred dollars on the strength so I didn't have to go into work and we began to look for things to get into.

The next day we had to return to the airport to pick up Beard's luggage which had been delayed so we all packed into a cab and headed out. Meko and I sat in the front seat and Sway, DoRight, and Beard sat in the back. On the way to the airport our cab driver, who was African, spoke to Meko in French telling her how pretty she was and asking her for a date as the rest of us, who didn't speak French, wondered what they were talking about. Ironically she told him I was her boyfriend so he would leave her alone. We picked up Beard's luggage, took it back to our apartment in the cab, and then we went to Spelman to visit Melanie and Meko's friend Jennifer. When we got to Spelman we were directed to Melanies's room by security. Melanie told us that she really didn't get along with her roommate so when arrived we were expecting the roommate to be a little rude. We were right. When we got there Melanies's roommate was acting rude and talking real bad to Melanie. Eventually Beard couldn't take it anymore and began to rank on the girl so bad she left the room in tears. We, on the other hand, were laughing so hard that my face and stomach hurt. When we got over this episode we found out that Spike Lee was having a party to celebrate the launch of his latest movie School Daze so we made plans to attend. After walking around the college campuses for a while we decided to take the Marta to Lenox mall. We hung out at the mall for a while as Sway purchased a few items to wear to the party later that evening. We then took Meko back to Spelman to meet up with her friend and we returned to the apartment to hang out, get high, and get ready for the party. I had a little 25 automatic that I carried and Sway brought a 22 so at some point we began to hang out of window and shoot into the sky. It was a wonder we didn't have the police knocking at our door.

    After acting up for a while we got ready for the party and headed out. We hopped into a cab and went over to the venue where the event was being held. The place was huge and it was packed. There were several levels of what appeared to be an entertainment complex and there were young black people everywhere. I had never been to a party like this and I assume Sway, DoRight, and Beard had not either. We walked around for a while admiring all of the beautiful young women and enjoying the atmosphere. We eventually ran into Meko and her friend who had come separately with a bunch of girls from Spelman. The party was live and we kicked it late into the night.

    The next day Sway decided that he was tired of taking cabs and the MARTA and he wanted to go home and get his car. I had already quit my job at Wendy's so I decided that I was going as well. For some reason DoRight couldn't go so Sway, Beard, and I headed to the airport where Sway bought one way tickets to Seattle for all of us.

    When we got to Seattle my brother Doobie picked us up in Sway's ride. Sway drove a brown Chevy Bronco on 13inch Dayton's with major beats. We hopped in the car and headed over to Sway's house where he grabbed a few thousand dollars out of his safe and packed a small suitcase with clothes. We then went to a hotel where we rented a room. Beard couldn't go back to Atlanta so we took him home. Instead my brother was going to ride back with us. We chilled out in the hotel room overnight and mapped out a route back to Atlanta. Later in the evening a few girls came over and I hooked up with one who liked me throughout high school. I did my thing and then we went to sleep. The next day we said goodbye to the girls and we hit the road. We drove rapidly to Atlanta, alternating driving responsibilities and only stopping for gas. We would grab food from the gas station and hop right back on the road. We ended up driving to Atlanta in 45 hours nonstop but for gas. Once we arrived we went back to the apartment where DoRight was chilling. For the next couple of days we drove around the city checking out our surroundings. Sway was interested in the drug trade, however, DoRight and I had been following the news and we were well aware of all of the damage that the Miami Boys had been kicking up in the area. So we were more cautious about trying to set up shop in this city. After a few days of kicking it we decided to drive back to Seattle. This time DoRight was coming with us. We hopped on the road, alternating driving responsibilities again. I did most of the navigating since I was good at reading maps. One time I woke up to find that DoRight had gone the wrong way and taken us about 100 miles in the wrong direction. I quickly got him on a highway that would get us back on the correct route but this detour would cost us time and we ended up taking 48 hours to get to Seattle on our return trip.

It was the end of February 1988 and we were back in Seattle. I had no intentions of staying but I needed more money and the dope game was the most lucrative trade I knew. Kenyatta purchased a convertible beetle with her settlement money and rented an apartment in the neighborhood where I used to slang so we quickly reconnected. Her spot was nice and only a few blocks from the houses where I sold dope so I figured I would stack a few thousand dollars and then move back to Atlanta. K, who was about 3 months pregnant at this time, decided that she wanted to move with me and so I copped a pack and started hustling.

Initially I ran around with my crew smoking weed and sitting in houses alternating sales. But when I returned to Seattle I also began to smoke crack again. I hadn't smoked anything but weed in Atlanta but having access to so much crack quickly caused me to resume my occasional puff sessions. At this time I was what we called a 'closet smoker,' someone who puffed but didn't want people to know. Unfortunately, or fortunately depending how you look at it, you cannot hide a crack habit for long. At one point DoRight commented that I looked like I was losing weight. I ignored him but I knew that I was smoking crack a lot more these days.

About two weeks after returning to Seattle I caught my first felony case. I had been in jail several times but never for a felony. My brother, Greg, and I were hanging in the valley at Bruce's house when Sway pulled up in his Bronco. We asked Sway to take us to the store but instead he threw me the keys and said I could drive the truck. Doobie, Greg, and I hopped into the truck and pulled off heading to the neighborhood store we called Mr. Lee's. We would later find out that Sway had just shot up Cherry Street where the Crips hung out and the police were looking for his vehicle. We got to the store and I parked the truck in front. After purchasing a couple of 40's I was heading back to the truck when I saw my brother playing with a remote controlled car in the street. A neighborhood kid let Doobie drive the car and he was engulfed in making the car do all kinds of tricks.

"Let me try Doob," I said.

"Wait," he said, "I'm trying to do something."

I waited for a couple of minutes and then asked again.

"Let me try now, I'll give it right back."

"Hold on," he said.

"F*** that, I'm leaving," I said as I got into the driver's seat of the truck.

As I was about to start the Bronco I looked into the rearview mirror and saw a police car pulling up behind me.

"Put your hands out the window," the officer commanded over the loudspeaker.

My heart began to race. I had my 25 automatic in my coat pocket and about $100 worth of crack in my pants pocket.

I opened the door and acted like I didn't hear him.

"Freeze," I heard him say as I began to quickly walk toward the store.

"Freeze," I heard him say again as I ducked into the store.

I quickly went to a back aisle and hid the gun but before I could get rid of the dope the officer had entered the store with his gun drawn and was ordering me to lay on the ground with my hands behind my back. I was cuffed and led out of the store as more back up officers arrived. They searched me and found the dope and searched the store and found the gun. As I was being placed into the patrol car I looked up and saw Sway on Greg's porch watching. I was taken to the precinct and booked.

I was sure I was going to prison and I began to prepare my mind for what I expected was the inevitable. I called K and told her what had happened. I told her I loved her but I would probably be going away for a while. I then began to do jailhouse workouts to get in shape. After 72 hours in jail, I went to court and I was told that I was being released. They had not filed charges, instead they were reserving their right to file charges and I was being released under investigation of VUCSA. VUCSA stood for Violation of the Uniform Controlled Substance Act. I was out of jail after being sure that I was going to prison and I decided I was not going to wait around and wait for them to decide to press charges. I hooked up with a cat from California and began moving ounces on the block trying to make as much money as I could as quickly as possible.

One night I was on the corner of Madison moving work outside of the corner store. I had about $300 in one sock and $300 in my pocket. I had a quarter of cut up rock in my hand and a solid quarter in my other sock. I was on the block alone for about 20 minutes and I had already made about $150. It was the first of the month so my plan was to move all the work I had on me that night. Originally I was just walking to the store from the house I was working out of to get some beer and let smokers know where I was but when I got to the corner I was rushed by about 4 customers so I decided to hang out for a second and see what was popping. I just finished making a $50 sale when I saw a police car come around the corner and accelerate towards me. I broke out immediately. There was a halfway house across the street from where I was so I ran across the street and ducked between the halfway house and the house beside it. I hopped a fence and cut through a few yards before coming out on the next street. I crossed quickly and ran between some more houses on the opposite side of the street. I paused for a second and heard sirens in distance. I ran across 23rd and Madison and ducked between some more houses as I headed south toward Union. About 7 blocks from the store I came out of the bushes and began to run down the street. I ran for four more blocks until I came to DoRight's house. I rang the doorbell and ducked as I waited for someone to answer the door. Soon DoRight came to the door and I quickly jumped inside the house. I told DoRight what happened and asked him to call me a cab. When the cab came I took a back route home. The store was right down the block from where K and I stayed so as we drove past I looked towards the store and saw 4 or 5 police cars on the block with lights flashing looking for me. I got home and went inside quickly and called it a night. I still had money to make but I told myself I was not going back outside tonight.

I hustled hard for another two weeks and then packed up K so that we could move to Atlanta. We planned on driving to Atlanta in K's convertible beetle while pulling her furniture behind us in a U-Haul trailer. But when we had difficulty trying to pull the trailer up a hill with the car we knew we wouldn't be able to tow the trailer through the mountains. So we put the household items in storage and hit the road. K's brother Ricky came with us when we left.

Their grandfather lived in Louisiana and he had recently become really sick so we planned on dropping Ricky off in Louisiana on our way to Atlanta.

In the last week of March of 1988 we hit the road. I remember listening to Keith Sweat's Make it Last Forever album as we drove cross country. We were not able to drive as quickly on this trip as we had in the Bronco because K's classic beetle was just not up to it. We stopped several times per day and stayed overnight in motels. It took us about three days to get to Louisiana to drop Ricky off. After staying a couple of days in Louisiana K and I continued on to Atlanta. When we got to Atlanta we went straight to the apartment DoRight and I rented. I made payments from Seattle so our lease was still in good standing. K and I moved in and I prepared for fatherhood, the next chapter in my life.

I had no intentions of selling crack in Atlanta so I immediately began looking for a job. I didn't want to go back to Wendy's and I didn't know if they would hire me back anyway so I looked elsewhere for employment. The first job I found was selling toys and other items door to door. We would meet at a warehouse and the management staff would go through these exercises to get the sales staff all excited and hyped and then we would ride out to a neighborhood in a company van where we would go door to door selling various items. We were paid a base salary with a bonus if we reached a certain quota. After about a week of this, and dozens of refusals, I decided that this was not the job for me. My next job was as a construction laborer. The job was ok and the pay was good but I only lasted a couple of weeks because I couldn't stand working for the owner's son who was the foreman of the sight. He was about 25 and he had a habit of doing dangerous things on the worksite and thinking they were funny. One day he was trying to convince us that diesel fuel was not flammable by lighting his lighter and smoking cigarettes next to the diesel fuel tank. He did a number of other silly and dangerous things but I decided to quit when, while laying pipe, he decided to shake the bucket of the backhoe over my head while I was in the ditch doing some work. He had done this to other laborers and they laughed it off as he sat on the equipment and laughed about the dirt that was falling on the workers. This wasn't funny to me and I told him not to do it again. When he did do it again I told him that I quit and he was lucky I didn't beat his a** for what he'd done. I left pissed off because the money was pretty good but I figured I would probably end up hurt if I stayed on the job with such a stupid and careless employer. I finally found a job that was right for me when I applied for a furniture rental company. I got the job but it was in Marietta, Georgia which is about 35-40 minutes north of Atlanta. K and I decided it would be better if we moved closer to my job so I found an apartment in Marietta, Georgia about a mile from the furniture company. In the beginning of April K and I rented a truck and moved our few belongings to our new apartment. Now that I had a good job I could relax a little. I went to Freaknik and reconnected with some cats from Atlanta who had gone to Grambling. K and I also went to a free concert in the park that featured Tony, Toni, Tone and Al B. Sure.

I was happy to start work as a driver for Cort Furniture Company. I was responsible for picking the orders from the warehouse, loading the truck, and delivering the items to the various customers. I was paired with another driver and together we would have anywhere from six to ten deliveries per day. We delivered furniture all over the Atlanta area but mostly in the northern region and the smaller cities near Marietta. K and I were doing pretty good around this time. We had a little pool at our apartment complex and on warm days I would teach K how to swim. She was almost six months pregnant and showing a lot. After work I would spend a lot of time hanging out with my upstairs neighbor. His name was Cochran and he was an older gentleman who lived with his girlfriend and his cute daughter who was about my age. Cochran was a metal worker. We would sit out on his deck and drink and smoke weed while playing cards and just chilling. Sometimes Cochran would barbeque and K and I would go up there to eat and hang out. Life was pretty good for a few months as K and I settled in and prepared for the birth of our child, but things were about to change.

On July 1st, 1988, my birthday, K's family member arrived. She came to help K with the baby so we were both happy to have her initially as she would cook dinner and help K around the house in other ways. On August 14th, 1988 my daughter Malia was born at Grady hospital. My mom and my nephew Alvedo came out from Seattle to see Malia and stayed for a couple of days. Malia was a beautiful little girl and I loved coming home from work to play with her. Over time I began to notice a different dynamic in the house. Our guest wasn't working so she was always at the house. We only had a one bedroom apartment so there wasn't much room for three adults and a baby. Three or four months after Malia was born I began to ask K how long our guest planned to stay. This began to be a serious point of contention between us and we ended up fighting a lot. K seemed to want the guest there indefinitely and I had decided that it was time for the guest to go so that K and I could focus on building our own family unit. Over time our fights became more and more heated as we argued over our household situation. I began to seek some sort of solace away from home and one day I struck up a conversation with one of the salesmen at work.

I noticed this guy before and I would often make small talk with him. He was an African American man maybe ten or fifteen years older than I was but what drew me to him was his attitude. He was always optimistic and positive. Whenever I saw him on the job he had a smile on his face and something nice to say. As I remember this part of my life I regret that I cannot remember the gentleman's name because I would very much like to track him down and tell him how great a part he played in changing my life. For as it turned out on this particular day I began to share with him some of the problems I was facing at home. I told him that I was trying hard to be the father I was supposed to be but my girlfriend just didn't seem to want to work at building a family where she and I and our daughter was the focus. I told him about our fights and my frustration with her mother's continued presence and I told him that I was at a breaking point where I didn't know if I wanted to keep doing this.

Then he told me about Jesus. He told me that God loved me and it was his intention for me to be the man that I was intended to be. He told me that the enemy wanted to destroy my family and he would try to do it by removing me. He told me that God so loved the world that he sent His only begotten son that whosoever believeth in Him shall not perish but have everlasting life. And then he asked me if I wanted to accept Jesus Christ as my Lord and Savior. He explained that when I accepted Him Jesus Christ would began to help me with the difficult situations I was facing. He told me that the Holy Spirit would help guide me and direct me in making decisions that were beneficial to my wellbeing. He also told me that with Christ I would never be alone because God would never leave me nor forsake me. All of this sounded like exactly what I needed and there was something else that I could not explain that drew me to talk with this man on this day. So right there on the loading dock, during our lunch break he prayed for me and I accepted Jesus Christ as my Lord and Savior. After our prayer I immediately felt a sense of calm and release around my situation with K. It wasn't as heavy as it had been earlier. I felt much better and I was glad I had met this man and given my life to Christ. He then told me about his church and invited me to come out and worship with them. It had been a while since I went to church but I told him I would and he gave me the address before we headed back to work. I wish I could tell you that all of my problems faded away the moment I accepted Christ but that wouldn't be true. On that day God began something in me that has slowly come into fruition over many years through many trials and tribulations. On that day a seed was planted. That seed has continued to grow and as I write this book God is still working things out in me, but nevertheless, on that day my life was changed and I can look back now and see the significance of that moment.

But I still had demons to battle.

In December I took Malia home to Seattle. She was only four and a half months but she did great on the plane and was no problem at all. When I returned home after a week in Seattle K decided she wanted to find a job. She felt that since the guest was still with us she could watch Malia while we worked. Even though I was ready for the guest to be gone I didn't argue. I had started going to church with my coworker so that was helping me find different ways of dealing with disputes. I also figured another income would help out. K found a job working in a hotel a few blocks from our home. She was hired as a hostess so her responsibilities were welcoming customers to the hotel and checking them into their rooms.

With her job K seemed to gain a new sense of independence. During moments of disagreement she was quick to say, "I don't need you," or "Get on." I would ignore this and continue to try to do what I thought was best for my family. During this time I was also reading the Bible more and trying to get a better understanding of what it meant to be saved. K was a Jehovah's Witness so she would occasionally invite other Witnesses over to the house to try to teach me about what they described as "the truth." This didn't start until after I received Christ at work and began going to church but I didn't mind because I enjoyed the conversations about God and faith. I would often have questions that neither K nor her guests could answer and the next week a new witness would show up and attempt to better explain "the truth." There just seemed to be too many inconsistencies in their explanations and the focus seemed to be more on their religion then on Christ. I felt as if they were exerting more effort into trying to get me to become a Jehovah's Witness than to help me understand how wonderful Jesus was and how God Almighty had a plan and a purpose for me. I even visited a kingdom hall with them on one occasion but there was something about the strict religiosity of their faith that I was unable to reconcile with my own search for God.

Out of the blue, K came home one day and said there was a guy at her job who was going to help her make some extra money by selling dope. I had not been around any dope my whole time in Atlanta and I hadn't even thought about selling drugs as I felt we were doing ok with our two jobs. But in spite of this the first thing that came to my mind was, "I know how to sell dope, what do we need this cat for?" So before I knew it I was in an apartment complex up the street from our home asking some young brothers where to cop some crack. I spent about $30 and then waited until I saw someone who looked like they might be a smoker. I watched as a dude came up and bought something from the cat I had gotten my work from. As he began to walk back in the direction he came from I caught up to him and asked him if he had a spot.

"Yeah, I got a spot," he said. "What are you going to give me to let you in."

"I'll give you a $20 for every hour," I said.

"That's cool, come on," he replied as he continued on.

The cat's name was Eric and he had a two bedroom apartment in the complex with another dude named Nick. There was also a dude named Ray that was there but he didn't live there. Nick was ill with some sort of sickness that affected his muscles so he seemed tired a lot. They both worked in the kitchen of a cafeteria in Marietta. The apartment was dark and quiet. I didn't go into the bedroom but there was absolutely no furniture in the living room. We walked in and Eric said I could sit on the floor. As he sat down against the wall Nick came in. Nick was carrying a can and I soon found out that they didn't have a pipe to smoke out of so they used an aluminum can with tiny holes punched in the sides. They put cigarette ashes over the holes to act as a screen and then they put the crack on top of the ashes. They would then put their mouths on the opening of the can that you drank from and inhale as they lit the crack with a lighter.

I gave Eric a $10 piece of crack and watched as he took a hit. He seemed to get an enormous amount of smoke from the can. After he took a hit he passed the can to Nick who took a hit as well. Then Nick passed the can to me.

When he passed me the can I didn't think at all about the fact that I had given my life to Christ and was studying the bible trying to better understand God. Immediately I began to think about the hits I had taken in Seattle. The crack I had purchased was different from what I was used to in Seattle and I wondered what it would be like to take a hit from can.

So I took a hit. But something was different.

Instead of the sense of euphoria that usually accompanied a hit I began to feel guilty and paranoid. I began to think about how ashamed I'd be if K found out I was smoking or if I lost my job behind this. Several thoughts began to run through my head and I was unable to speak. Something had definitely changed but I didn't know it at the time. I was no longer able to just casually get high and go about my business. Crack began to affect me different. I didn't know that I would no longer be able to do what I had done prior to accepting Christ. I thought I could do what I had been doing in Seattle. Get high while making money. But over time I would learn that this was no longer an option for me.

But I didn't know that then, so I took another hit. Trying to get that feeling I had experienced in the past.

After we had each taken a few hits Nick offered me some beer. I eagerly took a glass. I didn't know if they were open to letting me sell out of their house but I figured that if they smoked then they probably knew other people who smoked. After that first night I would come through every week or so and just chill and get high and see if any customers came through. One time I even took K and the dude that worked with her. He gave Eric a piece to sit in the house for a while and Eric and Nick went into the back room while the dude, K, and I sat in the living room. After about an hour or two with no customers coming through the dude decided to leave. K and I hung out for a little while longer and then we left as well. I didn't smoke any crack while K was around because I didn't want her to know that I got high. One time she came over to the apartment looking for me and I jumped off the balcony behind the apartment so that she wouldn't see me high.

Over time I began to spend more and more time over Eric and Nick's apartment. Eric and Nick were cool and even though I sometimes felt a little paranoid I was able to chill while getting high. They were good people and I didn't get the sense that they were scheming or trying to get over. Eventually I realized that I was not going to be able to sell anything and we would just get together to get high. Sometimes a couple of girls who worked with them would come around and I found out that one of them was Eric's girlfriend. The girls smoked too and we would all sit around the living room taking hits and drinking beer until we ran out of dope.

At home K and I began to argue more and more. K had made a few friends at work and she began to hang out with them, and her relative was still living with us. Malia was now nine months old and walking and K's relative had moved in with us a month and a half before Malia was born. One morning we argued before I went to work and I decided I'd had enough. After work a coworker named Deon gave me a ride home. Deon had a truck, a little Nissan with rims and beats. When we got to the apartment I began packing up my stuff and loading it unto the truck. I took all of my clothing and belongings and some of the living room furniture. I needed the couch because it was a sofa bed and I took another big comfortable chair that was in our bedroom. K yelled and cussed the whole time I was loading stuff unto the truck but she never once asked me to stay. I probably would have if she had asked. I wanted to feel needed and appreciated and I didn't feel that way around her. So I left. I had a friend named Rob from Seattle who was also living in Atlanta. I talked to him about my situation and he said I could come and live with him for a while. So Deon and I took my stuff to Rob's and I moved in.

K and I still talked after I moved out. I would go by the house and check on Malia often and sometimes K would bring her by Rob's. I bought a little Mustang so that I could get around and I started working part time after enrolling in the Atlanta Art Institute. I wanted to be a sound engineer so I began taking classes. I also started dating this woman from my job. She was a little older than me but she was cute, so we hooked up a couple of times.

But my life was unraveling in spite of my attempts at maintaining appearances. I was smoking crack every time I got paid and I was missing classes and coming to school high. I was also putting myself in dangerous situations. I located a source for crack in the Bankhead projects in Atlanta where I was able to get twice the amount I would pay for in Marietta so I would drive the 30 minutes or so to cop and then go back up to Eric's apartment to get high. I would often go alone and on one occasion I decided to go to take a hit in the apartment of the dude who turned me on to the dealer. This dude lived in the projects right as you entered in with windows that overlooked the parking lot. It wasn't his house though because he lived with his mom and a few siblings. For some reason on this day after spending about $70 and getting about $200 worth of crack I decided to go to his apartment to take a hit before heading back up to Marietta. We entered the apartment and he introduced me to his mother and sister. We then went upstairs to a room where he said it was cool for us to get high. I gave him a piece of one of the rocks and I broke off a piece for myself. He took a hit first and then passed me the pipe. After letting the pipe cool down I put my piece on and took a long slow drag. While I was doing this he had gotten up and was looking out the window. As soon as I let my smoke out and was feeling the full effect of the hit he turned towards me and said,

"Oh s***, the police are out there looking at your car."

When I got up to go look out the window he said,

"Don't look out the window they're looking this way."

I didn't know what to do. I had a bunch of dope on me and I had just taken a hit so I was super paranoid. He tried to get me to give him the dope so that he could hide it but I wasn't that high. I went into the bathroom and locked the door. I took the back off the toilet and put the dope in there then I began to run water in the tub and got butt naked and got into the tub. I figured if the police came in I could play it off like I was just taking a bath. After about five minutes of this I realized that I wouldn't want to be butt naked if someone tried to run up on me so I quickly got out the tub and got dressed. I sat on the side of the tub with the water running for a while and tried to figure out what I was going to do. Finally I decided that if they were coming I would just have to run and ditch the drugs or something. So I collected my dope from the back of the toilet and came out of the bathroom. Dude had been knocking on the door for some time and trying to get me to come out so he was surprised when I opened the door. I immediately went over to the window to look and didn't see any police. After looking out the window I gathered up my courage and left the apartment as quickly as possible. The dude was trying to convince me that it was cool to stay but I had figured out that he was probably trying to get over and I wasn't having it. I broke him off a piece, hopped in my car, and cut out.

Unfortunately I didn't learn my lesson from this episode. I went back to cop something one day and this same dude disappeared with my $70. I figured I could let him walk with the money since I knew where he lived but after waiting for about 30 minutes I knew that he had run off and was probably somewhere getting high. The next couple of times I went down there I would ask if anyone had seen him and I said that I would pay someone if they could take me to him. In my stupidity I didn't realize that this was his neighborhood and he had more back then I could possibly have. So one night Eric, Nick, and I went down there to pick up something and by this time people began to recognize my car when I pulled in. As soon as I got out a dude came up to me and said he could take me to the guy I was looking for. I didn't know this dude but for some reason I said ok. I didn't even ask Eric or Nick to come with me. I just told them to wait for me in the car. I was smoking and drinking that day so I definitely was not in my right mind. I followed this dude down a path next to the apartments until we got to an abandoned apartment. All of the windows were boarded up but the door had been kicked in so people could go in and out. The door was off the hinges and just leaning on the doorframe so we had to kneel down in order to get in. Inside it was pitch black and I couldn't see anything in front of me. I lit my lighter and began following this dude throughout this abandoned building all the while asking if he was sure the guy I was looking for was in here. We went through several rooms then we went up some stairs through a couple more rooms then back down the stairs. We went in a circle through what I think was the kitchen and we were just getting back to where we came in when out of the corner of my eye I caught the shadow of a figure to my left. I had just come to the end of a wall and the person was standing behind the wall ready to attack. Before I knew it he had swung a bat or something and hit me in the head with it. I felt like an electric shock had shot through my body. I fell back against the wall and found that I was in a closet. I don't know how long I leaned against the wall but I was able to see the door so I broke for the door and got out before he could hit me again. As I ran back towards the car I heard yelling and gun shots behind me. I jumped in the car and took off not looking back and not talking to Eric and Nick until we were on the freeway headed north. When I felt safe I told them what happened. I had a large knot on my head the size of a tennis ball cut in half. It was so big that I could actually grab it and move it around. But our night was not over. We went down there to get some dope which we obviously had not acquired so we went to another place. This place didn't have the size or quality of the place in the projects but we had to take what we could get and I was most certainly not going back to those projects ever again. We got some work then went back to the apartment to smoke. After it was gone I called K and told her someone tried to rob me and asked her to meet me at the hospital. At the hospital I was told that nothing was broken and they didn't think I had a concussion. They gave me an ice pack and told me not to go to sleep for a while. I thanked them and left. That night I told K I was ready to go back to Seattle. She had wanted to go back for some time and now that we were living separately it was more difficult for her to make ends meet. We decided that we would leave in the next few days.

We returned our rented furniture and moved out of the apartment. I gave Rob my car and asked him to turn it back in to the dealership. I told him he could drive it as long as he wanted but that I wasn't going to make any more payments on it. I let him have all of the furniture I brought over then I packed my few bits of clothing into the bug and K, Malia, and I hit the road on our way back to Seattle.

Alvedo, Mom, & Malia 1987

Doobie & Meko

Me in Atlanta apartment

Me, Doobie, Butchie, Neal, DoRight, Percy, Kelly, & Sway

Chapter 4

THE STREETS

The fear of the LORD is the beginning of knowl-
edge, but fools despise wisdom and instruction.
Proverbs 1:7

I returned to Seattle with K and Malia in spring of 1989. K and I were in Atlanta together for a little over a year and Malia was about 9 months old. My mom still lived in the apartment in Tukwila so K, Malia, and I went to stay with her while we figured out what to do next. I immediately began looking for a job. My time at Cort furniture was helpful and I was soon able to get a job as a deliveryman at a furniture company in Tukwila.

Excited to be back in Seattle I hooked up with my crew to go out and party one evening. I'd found a job and was supposed to start the next day so I figured I would go out with homies and celebrate my return home and my new job. Sway picked me up at my mom's apartment and we met up with Doobie and some friends at a club downtown. It was good to be home around friends and family. All of the homies wanted to buy me drinks to celebrate my return home but I declined because I didn't want to be hung over on my first day at work. Sway, however, got tore down and I ended up driving us to his house after the club. Sway said that he would take me to work in the morning so I claimed a spot on the couch in the living room and went to sleep. When I woke up in the morning Sway decided he was too tired to drive me to work so he gave me his keys and told me I could use his car. This was fine with me. At this time Sway was driving a grey Volkswagen Beetle. He took the back seat out and replaced it with speakers so the car had major beats. Unfortunately, on that morning I was unable to figure out how to turn on the system. It was already late and I didn't feel like going back into the house so I hopped in the car and began driving to Tukwila. I wanted to be sure to be on time for my first day of work. Sway lived in North Seattle and Tukwila was just south of Seattle so I hopped on Interstate 5 and headed south. I took the Southcenter exit and made a left. As I was headed east under the overpass I passed a Tukwila police car that was traveling in the opposite direction. I continued to drive and glanced in my rearview mirror. A jolt shot through me as I watched the police car make a U-turn and begin to accelerate towards me. The officer turned on his lights and siren and ordered me to pull over. There was an AM-PM gas station on my left so I pulled into there and turned the car off. I was waiting for the officer to come ask me for my license and registration when I heard more sirens and noticed the officer had not gotten out of his car. Instead, he had his gun pointed at me and he was on his walkie apparently calling for backup. Soon there were four police cruisers in the lot surrounding me and they were telling customers to move away from their vehicles and go into the store. I looked around and noticed that all of the officers had their guns drawn and pointed at me. The officer who pulled me over instructed to put both hands out the driver's side window and open the door from the outside. I quickly complied and stepped out of the car with my hands up when instructed. Two officers approached me cautiously with guns drawn. One held a service revolver and the other aimed a shotgun, both were pointed at me. Around me there were at least seven guns all with me in their sights. Once I was handcuffed and placed in a police car they began to search the Volkswagen. The officer whose car I was in was surprised to find out that my name was Martin. They thought that I was Sway because I was driving his car. This is why they came at me with so many guns drawn. Sway was known as a shooter by most law enforcement agencies in the area and by many of the heads on the street. When I realized that they had mistaken me for Sway I began to feel a sense of relief. Maybe they would let me go soon once they checked descriptions or other identifying features. This, however, would not be a day when I would return home. They ran my name and found that I had a warrant for my arrest in connection with the case I caught prior to my departure to Atlanta. Sometime during my absence the prosecutor filed VUCSA charges and I was now wanted for felony drug possession. I was taken to a Tukwila precinct and then transferred to the King county jail in downtown Seattle. I was booked into King County jail, given a red jumpsuit to indicate that I was facing a felony charge, and taken upstairs to the 8th floor.

This time I was sure I was going to prison. I again readied my mind for the inevitable and began to work out to get my body in shape. I figured if I was going to the joint I was going to come out swollen, or muscle bound. I remember showering while rapping 'Gangsta, Gangsta' from NWA and gambling for trays so that I could have enough food to bulk up. I was in the King County Jail for about three weeks when my public defender told me I was getting time served for possession. I was fortunate, they didn't find the clip for the gun and it was my first drug offense. I was placed on probation and let go. When I found out that I was only going to serve three weeks I reached out to the furniture company to see if I could still work for them. I told them that I had some prior parking tickets that I was rectifying and they agreed to let me come on once I cleared up my issues. It appeared that things were going my way.

When I got out of jail my mom had moved to a larger apartment in Kent and K and Malia had moved into a duplex in south Seattle on Ferdinand Street. I moved in with my mom and started work at the furniture company. Life was uneventful for a while. I would go to work and come home and check in with my probation officer once or twice a week. K and I were trying to work out our issues and raise Malia together so every once in a while we would hook up and try to do family activities like go to the park or the movies. After a few months of this I began to get restless for the street life. I was still used to faster money and the freedom to hang out with my boys and do what I wanted to do. Unfortunately, I didn't know that things had changed for me in a major way. I didn't realize at the time that God had begun to change me from the inside out. I was trying to return to a lifestyle that I was used to; however, when I gave my life to Christ God began to reshape me. I know this now, but at the time I was oblivious to the power of God and His process of renewal, restoration, and renewal.

One day at work I injured my back carrying furniture and was no longer able to work with the furniture company. Right before Christmas I received a settlement for the injury which I figured I'd use to reestablish myself in the game. I bought my mom a $300 watch and some $100 earrings for Christmas, took a couple hundred dollars, and hit the streets. I hit the streets intending to make money in the drug game but I soon found out that if I had dope I would smoke more than I sold.

During this time my brother was also living with my mom and he had a Chevy Malibu station wagon that he let me drive. I headed back to my neighborhood but much had changed. Some of the younger homies were slanging now but I didn't have the same connections that I once had. This was partly because I was no longer able to hide my drug use the way I had before moving to Atlanta. Without being able to hide my use I didn't want to go around people who knew me while I was using. My brother also told all the homies not to sell me any work. I began to remove myself from my crew and hang out more with people I didn't know. Without my connections I was only able to get "double up" for my money, which meant if I spent $100 I would only get $200 worth of work. This made it very difficult to turn a profit if I was smoking part of my supply. Over time the goal changed from making a profit to working just to maintain my high. When I ran out of work I began hustling to get more dope. Over time I became more and more scandalous while on crack and seeking another hit. I would run for other dealers at times or I would sell fake dope to unsuspecting customers. I even went through a purse snatching phase.

But all of this was in complete contrast to who I was supposed to be. When I wasn't on these drug binges I was seeking to be a better person. Where I at one time didn't feel remorse for the things I did now I would be racked with guilt when I sobered up and thought about how I behaved. I would go months without using while hanging with family and friends and then disappear for a week out in the streets. I didn't know why I couldn't stop smoking crack but I knew I wanted to and I knew in my heart that I was not meant to be out in the streets. But I didn't know how to stop.

Eventually I heard Mea was smoking as well. She and I had never smoked together because I would avoid her along with other people I knew when I was getting high. She started hanging with a girl from Seattle who was dating a Crip dude from California. They had access to dope so I assume at some point she decided to try it. Later in life she and I would smoke together but that didn't last long Because I didn't like to see how crack had changed her.

I started spending more time with K and Malia even spending the night over their house sometimes. One day I was over K's house and we were in the back bedroom. K's brother Ricky was there as well as K's roomate. At some point K and her roommate began to argue over something. This argument quickly escalated into a full blown yelling and cursing match so I stayed in the back room trying to avoid any involvement. It turns out that K's roommate was mad that K and I were lying up in bed together in her house. So not only was she mad at K but she was mad at me as well. As I lay in the bed naked K's roommate suddenly burst through the door and began to cuss me out. She was calling me all sorts of names when she suddenly lunged at me. Since I was lying in bed naked there wasn't much I could do to avoid her. She ended up grabbing my inner thigh on my right leg leaving a deep scratch from her fingernails. I jumped out of bed surprised. I figured that my leg wasn't the intended target and she had just missed inflicting serious and potentially permanent damage to my manhood. K jumped between us and resumed yelling at her roommate. Eventually her roommate left the room in a huff, yelling and cussing the whole time. I quickly closed the door and began getting dressed. While I was getting dressed K's brother came and knocked on the door.

"Yo Marty, you better get out of here," he said, "She's in there heating up cooking oil."

It turns out that K's roommate had planned on throwing hot grease on me. I didn't even try to go out the front door. I finished getting dressed and climbed out the bedroom window. I jumped down landing on my mom's car which I was parked in the back of the house. I got out of there as quickly as possible and told myself that I would never again put myself in a position where I might be harmed by that woman.

K and I soon broke up after that. Our relationship was pretty chaotic since Atlanta but I continued to try to be a family man for Malia's sake. Even with all of my drug issues I tried to always be there for my daughter. The final straw for K and I came when I went to jail for arguing with K after she hit me in the head with a phone. I went to visit her and and I were asleep on the couch when my sister called. Since I was asleep I didn't know my sister was on the phone. All of a sudden I was jerked out of my sleep by K hitting me in the head with the phone, yelling and telling me my sister was on the phone. I hopped up pissed and began yelling asking her 'what in the f*** did she think she was doing hitting me in the head with the phone?' We argued and yelled until I got fed up and left the house. Because of the noise the neighbor ended up calling the police who showed up after I left. During this time, when the police responded to a domestic violence call, someone had to be arrested. So even though I wasn't there they issued an arrest warrant for my arrest for misdemeanor domestic assault. Sometime later, while out in the streets, I was picked up on this arrest warrant. From jail I called K to ask her why she gave the police my name. I was upset because I knew that she didn't have to give them my name, she could have told them anything. At this point I thought we were still together. We fought a lot but we were still parents to Malia and I wanted to be there for my daughter. I was in jail for a few weeks going back and forth to court. I refused to plead guilty so I was planning on taking the case to trial. I also didn't think K would show up to testify against me. Every few days I would call K collect to see what was going on in the streets. During one of these calls we began to argue and she told me that she cheated on me with some other dude. I was devastated. It's hard enough being locked up, but it's almost unbearable when you're locked up and you get some news that you are unable to do anything about. I hung up the phone pissed off. I ended up getting into a fight with another inmate which resulted in me being sent to solitary confinement. On that day I cut K off in my heart. I cared for her as the mother of my child but I no longer loved her. From that day on she was just a chick that I had a child with. I spent another two weeks in jail fuming in solitary confinement and then I was released when K didn't show up for court. When I got out of jail I was single. Over time K and I might hook up every now and then but she was definitely no longer my girl and I had no intentions of being with her for the long term. She permanently lost her place in my heart.

It was also around this time that K's brother got shot in the stomach while he and I were fighting some cats from out of town. I had beef with a cat that I got into an argument with while in a store called Richlen's. Richlen's was where a lot of us would go to buy beer and find out what was happening on the weekends. One night this cat from New York and I got into an argument over something petty while we were in the store. A week or so later I was driving the Malibu with Ricky in the passenger seat headed north on Martin Luther King toward the Valley when I saw the dude on the corner of MLK and Jackson. I turned right onto Jackson and drove up on the curb and hopped out of the car.

"What's up now nigga?" I said as I approached the cat and the dude he was with.

Before I knew it the cat pulled out a chrome 357 and hit me in the left side of the head. I kept my feet and began fighting with the dude over the gun. At some point Ricky must have gotten out of the car and began to fight as well. Suddenly I heard multiple gunshots.

Pop, pop, pop,

Pop, pop, pop, pop.

I stopped swinging on the dude and broke across the street ducking between two buildings. As I looked back behind me I saw the two cats running back toward a house where a third dude had was shooting towards us. I waited for a minute and then cut through some bushes to get back on MLK. When I got to the street I saw Ricky heading towards me in the Malibu. He had gotten into the driver's seat and went up the street and turned around and now he was heading south on MLK from Yestler back towards me. I began to wave to get his attention and jumped back as he swerved across oncoming traffic and hit a tree a few feet from me. I ran up to the car to find that Ricky had fallen out of the driver's side door and was lying on the curb on his back.

"Marty, I've been shot" he said.

I looked at him and noticed a little hole in his shirt. I lifted his shirt and saw a little entry wound in his stomach just above his belly button.

"Call an ambulance" I began to yell.

People began to converge on us and one lady said she saw the whole thing and already called 911.

The ambulance arrived pretty quickly and they loaded Ricky on a stretcher. I was covered in blood from a head wound so they insisted that I go to the hospital as well. They weren't sure if I was shot so they wanted me to get checked out but I was fine other than a large gash on the left side of my head. Another ambulance arrived as the one Ricky was loaded on sped off towards Harborview. I asked a homie to bring my car to the hospital and I climbed into the second ambulance.

When we arrived at Harborview they rushed Ricky into surgery and I was taken into emergency so that they could look at my head. They washed the blood away and found that I had a large cut on the left side of my head that was bleeding profusely. The doctor quickly numbed the area and began cleaning the wound. After he cleaned the wound he stitched up the gash and a nurse placed a bandage on my head. He said that he would be back soon and they left me alone. After sitting alone for a minute I decided to leave. I didn't want to answer any questions and I definitely didn't want any police running my name. I quietly got up and slipped out of emergency. I met up with some of the homies in the waiting room and retrieved my car keys. There was a couple of carloads of friends following us prior to the fight and they saw the entire altercation. They told me that as I was fighting one dude the other dude hit me in the head with the gun. He then shot Ricky as he was getting out of the car. Some of them were about to jump in when a third guy came running out of a house shooting at them. That's when I ran across the street and ducked behind the building. After being shot Ricky jumped in the driver seat and drove away looking for me. This is when I saw him coming back down the street before he hit the tree. They knew that Ricky was taken to surgery but they didn't have any more information. After hearing this I went to my car and left the area as quickly as I could.

My head was spinning. I headed over to K's house to tell them what had happened. When I got there no one was there and I didn't have a way to contact them. I sat in my car for a while wondering what to do. I was worried that Ricky might die and I didn't know what to do. For some reason I decided to hide from the situation. I totally checked out and decided to go get high. I had about $50 so I went and got $100 worth of dope and I went to a crack house I knew of a few blocks from the hospital. I ended up staying out for about a week just drinking and smoking crack. I rarely ate and I would call friends and family occasionally to find out how Ricky was doing. I was told that he came out of surgery ok but he was still in critical condition. They said the bullet had done considerable damage internally but he was going to survive. I couldn't bring myself to speak with K or her family. I felt as if Ricky got shot because of me and I didn't know how to make the situation better. So I continued to get high.

After I smoked all of the crack I purchased I began to hustle to maintain my habit. I gave dealers rides and ran various errands. I rented out my car for a few $20 rocks and sold fake dope. After a few days on the block these methods were not so successful anymore and I had to think of another way to come up. There was one dealer who wanted to buy the Malibu, so at a particularly low point I decided that I would sell him the car for $300 worth of rock. It occurred to me that the car was still my brother's and he had only let me drive it but I had been up for days and I didn't care about myself or anything else, I just wanted to get high. I went to my mom's house when no one was there and got the title for the car. I then went back to the crack house and sold the car. After selling the car I went and sat up in a spot smoking and making the occasional sale so that I could purchase more dope to stay high. I stayed in the streets for about two weeks before I got up the courage to go home. Something within me told me that I couldn't hide from this forever and I figured that I had to face the situation head on.

When I got home I found out that Ricky was doing better and he was out of the woods. He was going to survive. I was very glad to hear this and it made coming home a little easier. K was pissed about the situation and she was inconsolable. My brother saw someone driving the Malibu and when he confronted them they told him that I sold it to them, so he was pissed at me as well. People were pretty upset with me for a while but in time my brother forgave me and as Ricky got better I was able to talk to him and apologize for the position I put him in.

After the shooting I was able to stay clean for a few months. My mom moved again and I moved with her. We moved back to Tukwila in some apartments overlooking Southcenter. My brother was expecting his first child and his girlfriend was always over the house hanging out. She and I did not get along at all. I was pretty close to my brother and it was as if she was competing with me in some way for my brother's attention. It was also about this time that Meko and I began to explore a closer relationship. Meko and I were friends for a number of years but we never took it any further than that. She knew about my relationship with K and she never did anything to disrespect that relationship. She also had a boyfriend that she was with for a while. We did not even consider a more intimate relationship until after I told her that I had broke up with K.

Meko carried herself well and she wasn't into a lot of mess, I respected her a lot for that. We began to hang out more and she would chill at my mom's with me watching movies and just hanging. She would also do my hair for me when I wanted it braided or put into locs. On Valentine's Day 1990 we hung out and got a little closer. Sometime during the night we heard doors slamming and tires screeching. When we went outside the next morning we found that Meko's car had been keyed. Meko had a new 1990 Honda Accord and someone took a key and scratched both sides of the car across the front and rear doors. I suspected it was K because she had quite a temper but we never found out who was responsible.

Slowly Meko began to take a special place in my heart. She was trustworthy and responsible and I could count on her to do what she said she was going to do. Meko also got along really well with Malia. K didn't like this at all but I was glad that they hit off and I felt that Meko was a good role for my daughter. Meko also got along really well with my mom which was a plus.

After a year in the Southcenter apartment my mom moved out to Federal Way and once again I went with her.

By the time we moved to Federal Way Meko was my main girl. I still struggled with being monogamous but she was who I considered planning my future with. K was fading further and further from my focus. On one occasion she came over to the house to visit my older sister and we got into an argument. My sister wouldn't make her leave so eventually I left to avoid an escalating confrontation. On another occasion K called while Meko was at the house. I finally had to tell her that I didn't want to be with her and Meko was my girl. After this K began to better understand that she and I were through. Part of it was my fault because I would still hook up with her every so often, but as I spent more and more time with Meko I better understood what I was looking for in a woman and what I was no longer willing to tolerate.

Meko was a good influence on me and she helped me look at life with a more optimistic perspective. I'd recently begun to reconnect with my dad and this was a relationship that Meko really encouraged. Through my experiences with K I realized that he might not have been totally at fault for divorcing my mom. Prior to my becoming a father I blamed him for leaving us. I now understood that sometimes it was necessary to separate yourself from someone who might be detrimental to your wellbeing. I didn't know the details of the relationship between my mom and dad but now I was willing to give him the benefit of the doubt. My dad lived about 45 minutes north of Seattle so Meko and I would take Malia out to visit him on some weekends. My dad was caring for his father, my grandfather, for a few years and when my grandfather died Meko suggested I ask my father if I could go to Chicago with him for the service. I really wanted to go but it didn't occur to me that he might want me to go or that he might enjoy my company on the trip. My dad did let me go with him even though I had no money to contribute to the trip. He bought me a ticket and we headed out to Chicago to transport my grandfather back to his city and plan his burial service. I got reacquainted with many of my family members from my dad's side and my dad and I had the opportunity to bond and develop a better relationship. I returned home happy that I had made the trip and I looked forward to spending more time with my dad.

Meko and I had a pretty good relationship but it was becoming more and more difficult to hide my drug use from her. For a long time Meko didn't know about my drug problem. By keeping my street life separate from my home life I was able to hide my addiction from her for a while. I worked at various jobs in food service or construction and tried to maintain certain appearances. But in 1993 a few things happened that made it much more difficult to hide my addiction. In January of that year my friend Sway was killed. The police found him in the trunk of his car at a park in south Seattle. I last saw him at a New Year's Eve party about a week before he was killed. Sway's death was very difficult for me. I began to really think about my mortality and what would happen to me if I died while in the streets committing crimes. A few months later another one of my friends was killed while we were downtown at a club. Some people came through shooting and a homie near me was hit in the foot. We found out later that the same shooters killed my friend behind the club and shot up the front of the club as they left. I lost about five homies to gun violence that year and it made it more and more difficult for me to avoid using drugs and alcohol to deal with the pain, anger, and hopelessness of my situation. This was perhaps the darkest period of my drug use. I stayed in the streets for days and then came home for about a week or two to recuperate. As soon as I regained my strength or acquired some money I would run right back out into the streets. I spent days in crack houses feeling guilty and too ashamed to go home or be seen by any of my friends or family members. Because of these feelings I would just stay out and away running with drug users/dealers like myself who made moves, not to get rich in the dope game, but to maintain a habit that was quickly becoming the focus of my life.

All of this started to present itself in my relationship with Meko. On a couple of occasions I neglected to pick her up from work. I dropped Meko off at work in the morning and then hit the streets in her car. After getting high all day I was so guilty or so worried that she might know I was using that I just didn't pick her up. I know now that this didn't help the situation, but like Rick James said, "Cocaine is a hell of a drug," and when you're under the influence there is no way that you're able to think rational thoughts. So I disappeared for days on end without explanation and then came home with some lie about where I'd been. I was also racking up a lot of jail time during this period of my life and I was having trouble explaining why I was in and out of jail so often. I went to jail for assault, driving without a license, driving with a suspended license, and possession. Over time with the accumulation of these incidents Meko began to suspect something was wrong and I could no longer lie about what I was doing. I had to admit to Meko and myself that I was struggling with cocaine addiction. After her initial disappointment Meko began to research treatment programs for me. I had never considered a treatment program before, my pride would not even allow me to view myself as having a problem, but with Meko's help I began to look at my behavior from another angle. She helped me schedule a drug assessment where I met with an addiction counselor to determine the extent of my addiction. After my consultation the counselor suggested that I go into an inpatient program as soon as possible. Because I wasn't working consistently I qualified for financial assistance at an inpatient facility just southeast of Seattle called Cedar Hills. During my street activities I violated my probation so my probation officer told me that to avoid further jail time I would need to do 90 days in Cedar Hills. I figured 90 days in a treatment center was better than 90 days in the King County Jail breathing recycled air, and being confined with a bunch of other inmates, so I agreed to do the three months. I also really wanted to stop using and I thought this stay might be helpful in combating this drug thing.

Cedar Hills was an interesting place. It was in Maple Valley, Washington located next to a dump which you could smell on hot days. There was a cafeteria and a building where clients could do art projects. There was also an administration building where the clients were processed when they arrived and before they were released. There was a women's dorm and two smaller men's dorms with meeting rooms in one of the men's dorm buildings. There was also a small weight room in the cafeteria building, a gazebo, and an outdoors basketball court. There were trails through the woods that surrounded the grounds and a few wide open fields for various activities. As clients we were required to participate in daily group meetings and classes. There were small group sessions as well as larger meetings once or twice a week when outside guests could come in and participate in the meetings. We could have visitors on Saturdays and Sundays and Meko or my mom would come out every weekend to bring me various treats like beef jerky or candy.

My stay at Cedar Hills was actually quite helpful. I began to get a better understanding of what I was dealing with and I got some tools to help me in difficult situations. I was told that addiction was a disease that I would be fighting for the rest of my life. I was told that in order to remain sober I must always be aware of my friends, moods, and surroundings. I learned a lot during my 90 day stay and I came out of Cedar Hills healthier with a more optimistic outlook on life. But I had not yet conquered my addiction and it would soon rear its ugly head again.

When I came home from Cedar Hills I got a job as a cook at Red Lobster near the Federal Way mall. Soon I found out that Meko was pregnant. She and my brother's girlfriend Leniece were pregnant at the same time and we were all excited at the thought of the babies being born around the same time. In her first trimester Meko had a miscarriage. We were both heartbroken and I did all that I could to comfort her during this difficult period.

I stayed at Red lobster for a while before I was offered a job as a bus monitor with the Seattle School District. The school district job was a pretty good opportunity. I caught a bus into Seattle in the morning and met my bus driver at the bus lot. I rode with him to pick up all of the students on his route and then took them to the African American Academy. I was responsible for maintaining order on the bus while we were in motion and preventing any distractions to the driver. Once the children got off the bus I was free to do whatever I wanted until school got out at which time I would meet the bus at the school to take the children home to their various bus stops. I enjoyed this job and I figured if I did well it might open up other career opportunities within the school district.

It was during my time with the school district that I found out Meko was pregnant again. When we found out she was pregnant we were both very excited. We waited for a while before telling anyone because we wanted to wait until she was in her second trimester and out of the high risk miscarriage period. When we safely reached that date we told our family members, most of which were as excited as we were.

Unfortunately my time at Cedar Hills had not completely cured me of my drug addiction. Although I was working steadily, every month or so, I would go on a one or two day drug binge after getting paid. There were a few dudes that lived near me in Federal Way that I hung with when I was getting high. Rob and Jazz were two brothers who lived in the apartment complex next to ours. Mace was a cat who grew up in the valley but moved to Federal Way. Stephen lived next door to me. The five of us would come up with different ways to get paid and then go somewhere to get high while thinking of new ways to get paid. Rob was a couple of years older than me and Jazz was a year older than Rob. Both Mace and Stephen were two or three years younger than me. Rob and Jazz would have these heated arguments where they would yell and scream at one another and call each other all kinds of names but they never got into physical fights. It was actually quite amusing unless we were trying to get something done and then it became irritating. I worked at the school district and ran with these guys on and off for a few months until Meko had to be rushed to the hospital.

At the hospital we found out that Meko had begun dilating five months into her pregnancy. The doctors determined that she had a weak cervix and must remain on hospital bed rest until the baby was developed enough to be delivered. This was quite a shock to all of us. Because of her condition Meko had to literally remain in the hospital for the remainder of her pregnancy. She was required to stay in bed all day every day and she even stayed in bed when they changed her bedding. I went to visit her between my morning and afternoon bus routes and otherwise tried to be there for her. But I wasn't always so nice. Sometimes I would call her spoiled because she got to lay up in the hospital all day and have friends, family, and hospital personnel cater to her every need. I was totally oblivious to the fears and concerns she was dealing with around the safety of the baby. I was too caught up in my own issues to be there emotionally for her the way I should have been.

I continued to work and get high on occasion until I got a call from the hospital.

After being in the hospital on bed rest for two months Meko began to go into labor. She was only seven months pregnant and there was much concern for the safety of the baby. I was out in the streets when I got the call but I rushed to the hospital and began to comfort Meko as much as I could. She was allowed to labor in her room for a while and then she was taken into a delivery room. I sat with her talking to her and comforting her as the doctors performed a C-section to deliver the baby. The baby was in distress and they didn't want to risk harming Meko or the child by attempting a natural birth. After a short while my daughter Milan was born. She was premature and only weighed 3pounds 6 ounces but she was beautiful. The doctors let me hold her to show her to Meko and then they took her and placed her in an incubator.

Several friends and family members were at the hospital. Some came once they heard Meko was in labor and others were already there taking care of Meko during her long hospital stay. The doctors made me leave the delivery room after the birth so that they could sew up the incision they made for the C-section. I went out to the waiting room to let everyone know that Meko and the baby were fine and then I headed to the room where they told me Meko would be brought to recover. Soon many of the visitors left so I was able to sit quietly alone for a while. Having just come off of a three day run in the streets I was exhausted, so when they brought Meko back to her recovery room I laid down and was quickly fast asleep. As I tossed and turned in my sleep I began to moan and cry out in anguish. This would happen to me on several occasions later in life and I now believe that my spirit was in some sort of battle with the demonic and destructive influences of the drugs I was using. A few years later Meko recorded me during one of these episodes and played it for me when I awoke. It sounded very scary. It was as if I was speaking in some sort of guttural language that consisted of shrieks and groans. The sound was similar to something you would hear on a horror movie but it was coming from me. Even my voice was unrecognizable. Since I was acting so erratic in my sleep Meko called a friend of mine named Karim and asked him to come up to the hospital. When Karim arrived they woke me up and Karim took me home to my mom's house.

Meko's C-section wound became infected so she had to stay in the hospital for an additional two weeks after Milan was born. Milan was kept in an incubator in the Neonatal Intensive Care Unit of the maternity wing where other premature babies were kept while doctors tried to help them get strong enough to go home. While Meko was pregnant and on bed rest she was at the University of Washington medical center, this is where Milan was born, however, soon after the birth they moved them both to Group Health in the central district. Meko was kept in a room in the main building while Milan was kept across the street. Meko walked through an underground tunnel to get to the ward where Milan was being held. Meko didn't like being away from Milan but it was hard for her to walk all the way to Milan's wing so I would go and sit with Milan and hold her so that she wasn't alone in her incubator. Sometimes I spent the night in a room on the wing that was provided for the parents of the children on the wing. After two weeks Meko was released from the hospital but Milan was not yet strong enough to go home.

Meko went to stay with her grandmother when she got out of the hospital. I was still working but I was becoming more and more involved in the Seattle street life. I claimed I was trying to make some money to care for my family but my addiction would not allow me to maintain a consistent work schedule or prosper in the drug trade. Eventually I lost my job because of missed days and I turned back to the streets completely. I fooled myself into thinking that I would be able to smoke and sell drugs the same way I once had and I hit the block. Unfortunately my plan was a total flop and after a day or two I was back to making petty moves to maintain my high.

One night I was on 21st and Union when a car rolled up looking for some work. I was high but I had a real $20 rock and a fake one. The passengers in the car wanted to spend $40 dollars so I served them what I had. I moved away from the car quickly and was walking back towards the corner when suddenly a black suburban came speeding at me from up the block. I turned to run in the opposite direction and saw that another vehicle had pulled up on the curb behind me. I instantly knew that they were cops and that they must have seen me make the last sale. I ran between some houses and ducked under a fence. I began to run between houses jumping fences and cutting through bushes trying desperately to get out of the area. When I thought I was clear I took the money the customer gave me and hid it under some bushes. Then I tried to hide. Before long I saw a light headed my way. The officer spotted me and began to yell.

"Get on the ground, get on the f*** ground" he yelled with his gun drawn.

I complied and lay on the ground face down.

"Put your hands behind your back," he yelled.

Once again I complied and he handcuffed my hands behind my back.

He then turned me over on my back and proceeded to pepper spray me in my face.

My eyes were immediately on fire and I was having trouble breathing.

"Why'd you do that?" I yelled.

"F*** you," he replied, "get up."

He pulled me to my feet and led me through the bushes and houses back out to the street. When we got to the street he called for backup. The pepper spray was burning my eyes and I had to keep spitting to try and clear my throat but through my squinting eyes I saw the suburban pull up on the curb. I was thrown in the back of the suburban and we skirted off towards the East precinct.

"That'll teach you to run, punk," the officer said as he and his partner laughed, "and stop spitting in here."

I was pissed. I was on my way to jail with a face full of pepper spray.

When we got to the precinct the officers took me over to a sink where I was allowed to rinse my face and eyes. After several attempts my eyes were still burning but it was easier to breath. I was then taken to holding cell where I waited to find out what I was being charged with. Thirty or forty minutes later I was handcuffed again and transported to King County Jail where I was booked. I found out that I sold to undercover officers and I was being charged with sales and distribution of a controlled substance, a felony. I wasn't sure how to react. I just had a baby and here I was facing prison. I was in a bad way and I didn't know which way to turn. So I began to pray.

I didn't pray because I was afraid of prison. I didn't pray because I felt God could get me out of the situation I was in. I prayed because I knew the person I'd become was not who I was meant to be and I needed help to climb out of the pit I dug for myself. Something within me was crying out. God began a process of change within me when I accepted Christ but I was still holding on to my old self. I was a new creature but I continued to function as if I could live any kind of way. I'd love to say that from the moment I prayed that prayer God did a miraculous move and I never used again, but that wasn't the case. God continued to slowly change me from the inside out meeting me where I was, but unfortunately I had not learned the necessary lessons needed to cause me to renounce my destructive lifestyle and surrender to Christ.

I stayed in jail for a few weeks until my family could bail me out. I was facing 63 months in prison and they had a strong case. I sold to undercover officers and they found the marked money I hid. Things did not look good but for some reason I had a sense of peace. Meko wasn't happy at all but she had my back. I returned home and tried to stay focused and sober.

It was very difficult to avoid the temptations of the street when I returned to Federal Way. My friends were still doing the same things and they would come by the house every once and a while to try to get me to hang out with them. But I resisted. Instead I focused on spending time with Meko, Malia, and Milan. My case was proceeding and I found out from my lawyer that I could take a plea deal and serve four months in a prison program called Work Ethic Camp instead of serving a much longer sentence in general population. I agreed to the plea bargain and pled guilty. Just like my lawyer promised I was sentenced to the four month Work Ethics Camp on McNeil Island. I was allowed to remain out on bail and given a date to turn myself in. Milan was growing and Meko and I were doing well. She was concerned with my upcoming prison stay but we were both encouraged by the fact I would only have to serve four months. Around this time I started praying and reading my bible more. One day for some reason Stephen's mom and I entered into a conversation about God. She was always talking about the goodness of God and encouraging us to do the right thing and go to church. I talked to her briefly about my experience receiving Jesus in Atlanta and told her that in spite of that I was still having a hard time staying crack free and out of trouble. She was quiet for a moment and then she asked me if I had received the Holy Spirit.

I was somewhat familiar with the Holy Spirit from my personal reading of the bible but I told her I did not know what it meant to receive the Holy Spirit. I was raised in a Baptist church and baptized as both a child and an adult and I knew the people in the church where I grew up talked about being filled with the Holy Spirit but I didn't know how to tell if I was personally filled with God's Spirit. She explained to me that we are saved when we give our lives over to Jesus Christ as I had done in Atlanta but it was the power of the Holy Spirit which equipped us with what we needed to stand strong and resist the temptations of the enemy. I knew I wanted to change and I didn't know why I kept falling.

"How do I receive the Holy Spirit?" I asked.

She told me that I must pray for it while the elders of the church laid hands on me. She then told me to wait while she went and made a few calls. We were sitting outside on the deck so I just chilled for a few minutes waiting for her to return. She and Stephen lived next door to us so our backyard decks were right next to one another. We were talking on my deck and she went next door through her sliding glass door to make the phone call. When she came back out the glass doors she was smiling from ear to ear.

"We're going to pray for you tonight at my church." She said.

She made arranged for me to come to her church that evening so that the elders of the church could pray for me and lay hands on my in order that I might receive the indwelling of the Holy Spirit. She told me to meet her in front of the house at 7pm so I could ride with her to the church and then she prayed that God would reveal Himself to me and fill me with His Holy and Righteous Spirit. After the prayer I went in the house and told my mom about our conversation and my plan to go to church later on to receive the Holy Spirit. My mom raised us in the church and she knew that I accepted Jesus in Atlanta but we never really had in-depth conversations about God. We were just expected to go to church so that we knew about God. When I told her I was going to our neighbor's church later my mom said she was going as well.

At 7 o-clock we went out to meet with Stephen's mom. We all piled into her car and she pulled off headed for her church. Her church was in a small building about five miles from our house. When we got inside I noticed two elderly men and three older women were already there. We entered the church and after some brief introductions they asked me to come up to the altar. They told me that they were going to begin praying for me and they wanted me to pray that God would fill me with His Holy Spirit. And so we all began to pray.

I began praying quietly but I noticed that Stephen's mom and the other women were moaning and rocking back and forth. My mom was sitting in one of the pews and she too was rocking back and forth praying with her eyes closed. The two men were standing on either me as I knelt at the altar. They each had a hand on one of my shoulders and they were praying in a language that I was not familiar with. At first I was nervous because I had never experienced anything like this before but every once and a while someone would tell me to pray harder because God wanted to endue me with power. I continued to pray and at some point the moaning and prayers of the people around me became less and less distracting. I could hear someone telling me to let go and let God have His way but I didn't know what that meant. Suddenly I was aware of an overwhelming feeling of what I can only describe as sadness. I began to cry uncontrollably as I knelt on my hands and knees in the front of the church. Tears were streaming down my face and snot was running from my nose as I began to cry out to God in guilt and anguish as all the thoughts of how I sinned began to fill my mind. I thought about all the people I hurt and the pain I caused my family and I began to beg for God's mercy and forgiveness. The prayers of the others began to sound like they were in harmony and I felt a pressure being released from my heart. I continued to pray and ask God to fill me with His spirit. I was aware of someone moving back and forth behind me and I kept hearing someone say pray faster. I continued to pray for God's mercy and guidance, for strength and forgiveness. My body began to feel tired but I wanted to continue to pray. At some point I noticed that I was no longer praying in English. I could hear myself speaking but I didn't understand what I was saying. My voice was strong and powerful and I was moaning and crying as I lifted my hands up to the sky. I was praying in tongues. The feeling I felt was indescribable. I was someplace else and I didn't want to leave. The pain and guilt were no longer overwhelming me and I felt a sense of strength and relief. I cannot adequately describe what I was feeling but I wanted to maintain that feeling. I continued to moan and pray in tongues until I collapsed on my face on the floor. I lay there for a while crying and thanking God before I again became aware of the other people in the room. Slowly the two men helped me to my feet and I walked over to one of the benches where I sat down. I wanted, with all of my being, to remain in the feeling that I was having. I knew that I was forgiven for my sins and I was at peace. As I began to become more aware of my surroundings I realized that it was almost midnight. It occurred to me that we were praying for more than four hours. The two men came over to me and shook my hand and told me to stay in God's word so that I would be equipped to fight the enemy. Stephen's mom and the other women came over praising God for his goodness and thanking Him for filling me with the Holy Spirit. There was no doubt in my mind that God was moving on me and I left the church tired but joyful with a pressing sense of humility. We got home and I thanked Stephen's mom for taking me to the church then I went inside to lie down. My mom was tired as well but I could see that she was excited and very happy. We didn't talk much that night but we did begin to talk about God and the bible more. I decided I wanted to read the entire bible and I began a few weeks before I was to turn myself in to jail. In the weeks before I went to prison I spent more and more time with Meko and the children and when it was time to turn myself in to do my time I was at peace. One week before Christmas in December of 1994 Meko took me to the King County Jail so I could turn myself in. I was headed for prison but I had never felt so free.

Me in Chicago

Meko

Meko in her Honda

Milan & Quijan

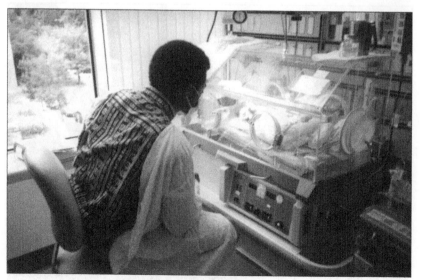

Milan in incubator

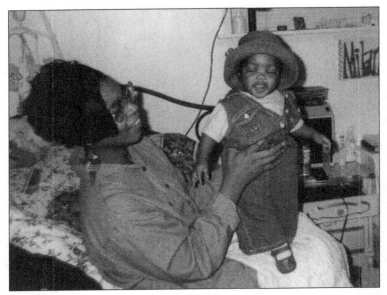

Mom & Milan

Tahdja, Terrence, & Tash

Chapter 5

INCARCERATION

Hear me when I call O God of my righteousness:
thou hast enlarged me when I was in distress; have
mercy upon, and hear my prayer.
Psalms 4:1

Almost immediately after turning myself in I was booked into the King County Jail, given a red jail suit, a pair of underwear, and a pair of rubber slippers, and transferred to the eighth floor. I was pretty familiar with the King county incarceration system by this time and I had an idea about what to expect. Over the years I was housed on almost every floor of the jail. The only floor I was not housed on was the psychiatric wing where they housed mentally ill and suicidal inmates. I was also familiar with the minimum security Northern Rehabilitation Facility, or Nerf as we called it. Nerf was a location were nonviolent inmates were housed in north Seattle. Nerf inmates had access to free weights, a full court basketball court, better food, and full contact visits. There were also weekly AA meetings, off site work duties, and women inmates who the male inmates got to interact with briefly at the AA meetings. Nerf was an open campus so if an inmate wanted to walk away he or she could. There was an occasional escape but inmates usually appreciated the opportunity to do their time at Nerf and didn't want to risk losing that privilege if they were ever incarcerated again.

When I turned myself in I expected to be in King County general population until I they transferred me to prison. My expectations were correct and I stayed on the eighth floor before I was called early one morning to pack up my belongings for transfer. I got up quickly and grabbed my belongings and the heavy blue mattress that I slept on. I threw the mattress on the pile outside the cell and placed my sheets in a laundry bin. I then went into the library to wait. Although it was called the library there were no books in there. If you wanted a book you had to catch the trustee who came around with books on a cart once a week. When I walked into the library there were already 3 or 4 men in there waiting to be transferred. We waited as more inmates were brought in and after about an hour there were about fifteen of us milling around. There wasn't much conversation unless you recognized someone you knew, but for the most part most of us were thinking about what was next.

I spent Christmas of 94 in jail away from Meko, Malia, and Milan. Milan was now six months old so I was eager to be transferred to prison, serve my time, and get back to my family. My four month sentence at the Work Ethics Camp didn't start until I got there so all of my time in the King County Jail and other parts of the prison were just extra time that I had to do. I was also ready to get out of the County Jail so that I could have access to free weights, better food, and fresh air. So I waited impatiently while the guards kept bringing in more and more inmates.

After being in the library for a little over an hour we were led out into the elevator and taken downstairs to another holding cell. When we got to the first floor holding cell we waited again as inmates from other floors of the jail were brought down to join us. We were then told to change back into the street clothing we were wearing when we were booked as the guards inventoried all of our personal property items and placed them in paper bags for the transfer. We were then taken to another holding cell. An hour and a half later there were about thirty or forty of us waiting to be transferred. We were all assembled in one room and then the guards brought each of a sack lunch consisting of a bologna and cheese sandwich, an apple, a small carton of milk, and a juice. I traded my milk for a juice then ate my lunch and continued to wait impatiently.

Soon I heard chains rattling and the door click. A Guard told us to file out into the hallway where there were other guards waiting with handcuffs attached to long lengths of chain. The guards wrapped chains around each of our waists and then cuffed our hand to the chain. They then cuffed our ankles with a chain that was about a foot and a half long. This caused us to walk with very short step. After each of us was sufficiently cuffed they paired us with another inmate and we were chained to them. I was paired with this cat from East Union named D.J. I didn't know him but when we started talking I found out that he knew my brother and we associated with a lot of the same people. D.J. was facing two years for a drug beef and was looking at doing the whole sentence. Later in life I ran in to D a few times on the streets and we would say what's up in passing. He eventually got life in prison for double murder. This caused me to consider the different directions our lives took from that point when we were chained together headed to prison. Now when I consider my life I often wonder why I was spared a worst fate.

We were led unto a large bus that was fortified with bars on the windows, metal eyelets on the floor beneath our seats, and a steel gate between the driver and the passngers. D and I shuffled awkwardly into our seat and then our feet were chained to the eyelets. When all of the inmates were seated and chained an armed guard boarded the bus, the bus doors closed, and we pulled out of the County jail garage headed south to Shelton, Washington. Shelton was the location of the Washington State Department of

Corrections Receiving Unit. This is where all of the inmates who went to state prison in Washington State began their time. It is from here that the inmates are classified and sent off to the various locations to do their time. It is also here where for a period of time hard core violent maximum security inmates intermingle with less violent minimum security inmates.

When we arrived at Shelton we were led from the bus and taken into a large holding cell. Our chains and hand cuffs were removed and we were taken to a meeting room where a correctional officer began to speak to us about the rules and expectations of inmates. We were then introduced to the warden who told us that this was his prison while giving examples of how hard he would come down on any trouble makers. He stressed how we were no longer on the streets, and therefore, we better learn to live by the rules he set here in his world. It reminded me of an old prison movie but I paid attention because I did not plan to get caught slipping by the guards or the other inmates.

One by one we were called up to a counter where our identities were confirmed. We were then given wristbands with our names and an identification number, mines was 955846. Throughout my time in prison the guards would identify me by my six digit number more than by my name. We were then taken to a room where we were told to disrobe. We were lined up side by side naked in a shower area and strip searched. We were told to lift our genitals up and then told to turn around and spread our butt cheeks to make sure we weren't concealing any contraband in our anus. After being searched we were led to another room, given state issued clothing, and paperwork with our housing assignments.

The prison at Shelton had two functions. Part of it served as the receiving unit, or R-units, where all state prisoners came to be classified before being transferred to the other state prisons like McNeil Island, Walla Walla, Monroe, Clallam Bay, or the other prison facilities and work camps throughout Washington State. Shelton also functioned as a correctional institution where inmates

144

could be classified to do their time. The R-Units at Shelton were just for male inmates. Female inmates went through intake and were housed in facilities in different cities throughout Washington, with the main one being in Gig Harbor.

I was sent to R-Unit 1. I followed the guard through a number of hallways and electronic doors until we arrived at the Unit where I would be housed. The door mechanisms worked in such a way that we all had to be inside a small space with the door behind us closed before the door in front of would open. There were guard stations behind thick glass where guards watched us on video monitors and controled the opening and closing of the doors. Each time a door was opened or closed there would be a loud click as large metal locks fell into place. I was somewhat familiar with this sound from my stays in the King County Jail but there was something different about this experience.

My unit was a row of cells on one side of a long hallway with several layers or tiers. At one end of the hall was a single shower stall that all of the inmates on that hall used at various times which they were assigned. The metal bars in front of each cell slid open when the guard, who was escorting us, called out the cell number to the guards in the control rooms. I was led to a cell on the ground floor about halfway down the hall and told to enter. The cell was about 8 feet by 10 feet with a bed, a desk and chair, and a metal toilet with a sink on the back of it where the water tank would normally be. I was pleased and surprised to find that I would be in the cell by myself. I placed my belongings on the bed and lay down to think. Christmas music was being piped into the cells from somewhere and I would soon learn that the same songs were played over and over for days and days.

I was here in prison and I didn't know what to expect. I had several friends who went to prison and came home to share their experiences but it was different being there myself. I wasn't surprised that I was there, in fact from the time I was 19 I totally expected to go to prison at some point, so this was not something that came as a shock to me. Unfortunately my choices and the environment I grew up in fostered a hopeless mindset within me that had me thinking that the only way to survive in a society that stacked the deck against me was through criminal activities. I didn't realize at the time that I was destroying myself and my community by doing exactly what I was being programmed to do. It was natural for me to want to resist the injustices I witnessed within American society but since I was not educated on how to properly work for change I became trapped in the system and labeled as part of the problem. As a felon I lost my right to vote and my right to bear arms. Through bad choices I'd forfeited my freedom and my rights and I was now unable to participate in the democratic voting processes designed to elect leaders who would make the laws that affected my future. Through my ignorance I removed my voice from the conversation and I became a non-factor and a statistic. I would have a lot of time to think in the coming weeks and I decided that I was not going to be corrupted further by this prison experience but instead I was going to use this as an opportunity to overcome some of the personal issues that were hindering my success.

After a couple of days it was pretty easy to fall into a routine. We were awakened at around 6:30 am with an announcement and a piped in bugle tune. After the bugle the piped in Christmas and New Year music began and continued until 10pm when the lights were turned off. At 7am we were lined up and led to the cafeteria where we were fed breakfast. Breakfast usually consisted of oatmeal or some other starchy substance, a meat item, a fruit item, milk, and juice. We had a certain amount of time to eat before we were led out to allow the next hall or tier the opportunity to come in and eat. There were maybe three or four tiers in the cafeteria at a time and I quickly identified a few people that I knew from Seattle. After breakfast we were taken back to our cells. We remained in our cells until 12pm and then we were taken back to the cafeteria for lunch. After lunch we could go out on the yard where there were a few concrete basketball courts and a large field with a track that ran around its perimeter. Inmates mingled around on the yard playing basketball, walking the track, jogging, doing calisthenics, or congregating in small groups talking and watching other inmates. I usually spent my time on the yard exercising. I would run laps and do pushups or play basketball. Basketball was more fun here than in the County Jail. In the County jail we had to play barefoot or in our rubber slippers. Here we had state issued converse type shoes so you didn't have to worry as much about stubbing your toe or otherwise injuring your feet. There were no weights on the yard and we didn't have access to weights during my first couple of weeks in the R-Units. After an hour on the yard we were taken back to our cells where we remained until dinner at 5:30. We were led to the cafeteria for dinner and then taken back to our cells where we remained for the evening unless it was our day to shower. We were made to take showers three or four times a week. Once or twice a week a trustee would come around with a cart of books. If we were behaving we were allowed to get a couple of books a week. Not surprisingly the selection was pretty similar to the books offered in the County Jail. There was a large selection of books by Donald Goines and other authors that wrote about pimping, drug dealing, murder, and street life. I began to wonder if these types of books were in part responsible for perpetuating criminal behaviors and recidivism in the inmate population. I'd read almost all of the Donald Goines books several times while incarcerated in the County jail and I usually came away from these readings with new criminal ideas and aspirations. I decided that I didn't want to focus on these topics while I was incarcerated this time so I looked for books that focused on positivity and hope. I also continued reading the bible in its entirety. I committed to reading passages from the Old Testament in the morning and passages from the New Testament in the evening. I would take breaks every hour or so and do sit ups and pushups and I would nap in the morning and afternoon. Before long I was on a pretty consistent schedule.

I also spent a lot of time talking to the inmate in the cell next to mine. He was in prison for murder after shooting up some cats who he had beef with. He was facing 20 to 30years and he was extremely stressed about his situation. He lost his first trail but was in the process of appealing the conviction. Strike was a tough looking cat with tattoos and I stocky build. He and I talked about some of our war stories and some of the people we knew in common but mostly I would encourage him not to be too stressed about his appeal. This was my first experience in prison with a cat who had a 'I don't give a f*** attitude on the street', but was not ready to accept the consequences of their actions. I would learn that even the hardest cats wished they had their freedom and would do things differently if they had the chance. Although there were some cases where prisoners became institutionalized it was rare that an inmate was content being locked up. Most of the inmates I talked to would not encourage their children or family members to follow in their footsteps. Even those inmates who might have been defined as institutionalized talked about helping their children avoid the mistakes they made. I quickly realized that prison was a place of hopelessness, hate, pain, violence, and despair and I didn't ever want to come back.

R-Unit 1 housed minimum, medium, and maximum security inmates which was how I, a minimum security inmate, was housed next to Strike an inmate imprisoned for murder. After a week in R-Unit 1 I was transferred to R-Unit 4 and Strike was transferred to another wing that housed maximum security inmates. He was classified to go to Walla Walla a maximum security prison in Eastern Washington that housed many of the state's most violent offenders. I was classified to go McNeil Island a minimum/medium security prison near Tacoma Washington.

I was moved to a two man cell that I shared with another inmate. My new cellmate was also convicted for a drug offense. R-Unit 4 was a minimum security wing where we were allowed more freedoms than R-Unit 1. We were allowed to play basketball on a real indoor court and we had access to a weight room full of free weights. We were given two hours of exercise time in the morning and two hours in the evening. The food was about the same and I didn't much like having to share a cell but overall the accommodations were much better than R-Unit 1.

While in R-Unit 4 I ran into a homie from the Valley. Shawn was a few years younger than I was and he was facing a few years for a drug offense. We were cool when we grew up but he became a blood when they came to Seattle so he began running with a different crowd. I'd seen him a few years earlier and he pulled a gun on me when he thought I was trying to rob him. For a while I would go to the Valley and ask my little homies who knew me as an OG to give me double up for $50 or $100. When they gave me the dope I would tell them that I owed them. They didn't like this but they still respected me in some ways even though I was smoking. I did this a few times before the word got out, then they would just tell me they didn't have anything when I asked. One night I came looking for work and I actually had money to spend. I knocked on the door of the house where the young homies were hanging and asked for a hook up. I knew they had dope but they refused to sell me anything. After a while Shawn came out and said he would hook me up. We walked the seven or so blocks to his house and I waited outside while he went inside. When he came back out he pulled a gun on me and told me that I wasn't going to jack him. I was pissed. I actually had money to spend this time and this guy walked me all the way to his house so he could get his gun and pull it on me. He didn't even have any dope. I called him a punk and showed him the money I was trying to spend and then I told him he shouldn't have pulled a gun on me. I didn't know what to think. Part of me knew he was right in his caution but the other part of me was pissed because I was trying to get high and this guy had wasted my time. So I left. I left pissed off and found some dope somewhere else. This was the last time I'd seen Shawn so when I saw him in prison I know he didn't know what to expect. When I ran into him I was back to myself and I had been working out for several months so I was in shape and back to my fighting weight. "What's up, Shawn?" I asked him when I saw him in the gym. "Nothing, what's up with you Marty?" He responded. "Nothing," I replied. We talked about what happened the last time we were together and then we squashed the beef. I wasn't mad at him. I knew that he just didn't want me to jack him and I knew that I put myself in the position where the younger homies couldn't trust me. So we squashed the disagreement and we were cool.

I stayed on this wing for about two weeks and then I was transferred to McNeil Island.

I was happy to be transferred to McNeil Island because the camp I was going to was on the island and I knew I was getting closer to starting my four month program. McNeil Island was a prison on an actual island in the South Sound near Tacoma, Washington. I was again shackled and loaded onto a prison bus that headed towards Tacoma. In Tacoma the bus drove onto a ferry that took us over to the island. We disembarked from the ferry and the bus drove up to the entrance of the prison. We waited until the guards inside opened the gate and then we drove into the prison and headed to the admittance center. We were led off the bus and taken into the building where we were unchained, classified, and sent to various housing units.

McNeil was very different from Shelton. The cells looked more like apartment buildings on the outside and they looked much newer. In the inside of my building there was a large common area where inmates were sitting at tables playing cards and watching television. Surrounding the common area were one man cells with sliding doors that had a window on top and a slot with a flap in the middle about waist level. There were two levels with stairs leading from the ground floor up to the second level. Over in a corner was a control room where guards were posted to watch the prisoners and control the cell doors. The inmates were also allowed to wear street clothes and have televisions and radios in their rooms. My cell was on the second floor so I carried my stuff up to where I would be housed and sat on the bunk.

When dinner time came we were allowed to walk over to the cafeteria on our own. While walking over I ran into a bunch of dudes I knew from the streets so I sat with them at dinner and they schooled me on what to expect on the island. When I got back to my wing I played a few games of spades and dominoes and watched a little television. Before lights out one of the homies gave me a few candy bars, chips, and a couple packages of microwave popcorn from his commissary and then I heard the guard yell, "rack back." This meant it was time to go back to your cell. I went into my cell and lay down on my bunk. I was excited to be at McNeil and I looked forward to getting the program over with so I could go home. I didn't know that I would be there a while before my time at the camp began.

I ended up staying in McNeil Island general population for almost a month before I was transferred to the Work Ethics Camp program. The Work Ethics Camp, or W.E.C., brought in new inmates at the beginning of every month to start the four month program, since I arrived after the first of the month I had to wait until a group cycled out.

I was required to work while in general population so I was assigned a job in the kitchen. I didn't do much cooking I mostly just broke down pallets of food and placed the items in their proper places in the kitchen. I went to the big yard when we were allowed and I went to the weight room four or five times a week. The big yard on McNeil Island was different than the one at Shelton. There was the field, the basketball courts, and the track but there were also free weights outside on the yard. The first time I went out on the yard I saw a lot of cats I knew from the streets. One dude came up to me to say what's up and I made small talk with him before intentionally breaking away from him to run some laps. I knew him from way back in little league football days but I also knew that a few years earlier he set up another cat in the drug game so that his sentence would be reduced. I definitely didn't want to be associated with someone who would participate in the game and then tell on someone else when they were caught. There is an old saying, 'Don't do the crime if you can't do the time.' This saying rings true. There are a lot of people who get involved in criminal behaviors without weighing the cost of those behaviors. So when they get caught they are unwilling to face the consequences and they end up saying or doing things to other people to reduce the weight of their consequences. This, by definition, is snitching.

While in general population I also saw a doctor and a dentist to make sure I was fit enough for the W.E.C. I checked out ok so I was given clearance to participate. I got into a routine and eagerly awaited the end of the month hoping and praying that I would be in the next group transferred to the W.E.C. My prayers were answered and on February first 1995 I was transferred to the Work Ethics Camp. At this time I'd been incarcerated for a little over two and a half months so I was excited to be starting the final leg of my prison experience.

I was taken over to the camp with a group of fifteen other guys. I didn't know any of them from the streets but there were some from Seattle as well as Tacoma, Everett and other western Washington cities. When we arrived at the camp, which was on the other side of the island, we were led into an administration building where we were checked in and given our W.E.C. uniforms. I was given a combination lock, a pair of converse like tennis shoes, a laundry bag, one pairs of sweat pants, one sweatshirt, three pairs of khaki pants, three khaki colored button-down shirts, a pair of black work boots, three white t-shirts, and three pairs of underwear. All of my clothing had my identification number stitched somewhere inside. We were allowed to keep the big state issued coats we were given at Shelton and three pairs of socks but everything else was taken. We were then led to a dormitory area where we were assigned bunks. We were in a large building with a cafeteria on the first floor and two large rooms with sleeping cubicles on the second floor. Each room housed two groups, or phases, of the program. The phase you were in indicated how long you had been in the program. My group was phase 1 since we just arrived. The group that was finishing up their last month was phase 4. As you graduated to a new phase you were given a stripe on the right sleeve of your shirts. Phase 1 had no stripes and phase 4 had three. My phase was housed with phase 4, while phases 2 and 3were across the hall. The sleeping area consisted of a wall that went down the center of the room. The wall did not reach the ceiling and you could walk around it on either end. The different phases were separated on opposite sides of the wall. Along the wall on both sides were cubicles that held a single bed and a cabinet where clothing and personal items could be held. There were about eight of these on each side of the wall. Across from these cubicles, near the windows, were two man cubicles that held a bunk bed and two cabinets. I was assigned to one of the single man cubicles. When you entered the room, before entering the sleeping area, there was a large meeting room to your right and a communal bathroom to your left. The bathroom had about ten sinks, ten shower stalls, ten toilet stalls, and several urinals. I placed my belongings in the cabinet and lay on my bunk. Soon we were called down for dinner and then we were allowed free time to get situated. We were told that our first day would begin at 6am and we must have our pants and shirts ironed. Some dudes from phase 4 showed us how we were supposed to iron our pants and our shirts, with creases in the front and back. After ironing my uniform I talked to some of phase 4 about the program and then went to my bunk. I sat alone thinking until lights out at 10pm and then I went straight to sleep.

The next day we were awakened at 6 am for physical training or P.T. The camp had a recreational building with a full court basketball court and a few meeting rooms. We were told to dress in our sweat suits and then we were taken to one of the meeting rooms. Here we were introduced to one of the correction officers who would oversee our stay at the camp and an inmate from phase 2 who would to lead us in the P.T. exercises. There were also female inmates there who were part of our phase. They were housed in another part of the camp but they did all of the camp activities with us. All together my phase consisted of about 10 men and 5 women. We started working out and for about an hour we did jumping jacks, pushups, mountain climbers, sit ups, cherry pickers, and other calisthenics in sets of 10 and 15.

"One, two, three," Our leader would count out and on the forth count we would say, "one" in unison. This went on until we reached the number that the leader called out at the beginning of the exercise. The call and response sounded something like this:

"Ten pushups are you ready?" the P.T. leader would yell.

"Yes" We would reply.

"Ten pushups are you ready?" The P.T. leader would yell once more.

"Yes" We would reply again.

"Take your position," He would yell.

We all got into the pushup position with our arms straight.

"Ready, Begin" he yelled.

"One, two, three,"

"One"

"One, two, three,"

"Two"

"One, two, three,"

"Three"

"One, two, three,"

"Four"

On we would count until we reached ten. We went down on the one count, up on the two count, down on the three count, and yelled out the set count on the four count.

"On your feet" The leader yelled at the completion of the exercise. Once everyone was on their feet he called out the number of the next exercise.

"Fifteen jumping jacks, are you ready?" And so on.

We did P.T. every weekday before breakfast. On most days we did P.T. in the same meeting room. Once or twice a week we would run a few miles around the island. Once or twice a month we would do an obstacle course that was set up on the grounds of the camp. The obstacle course was similar to obstacle courses used by the military during basic training. We got a pretty good workout from running through them so not everyone was able to keep up in P.T. or complete the course the first few weeks.

After P.T. we went to the cafeteria where we ate breakfast. The food was similar to the food in general population but we could go up for seconds and thirds if there was food remaining. After eating we were told to go back to our dorm, change into our uniforms, and meet back in the courtyard outside of the cafeteria by 8 am.

In the courtyard each phase was lined up in pairs of two. I found my phase and got into line. I looked around and noticed the stripes on the arms of the Phase 4 inmates and thought about how good they must feel to be in their final month. One by one the phases were led away to their different work details. My phase was told that we would be doing some forestry work and then we boarded a yellow school bus. The correctional officer, or C.O., in charge drove us over to a shed where we grabbed several tools, some shovels, rakes, leather work gloves, and a couple of chain saws. We loaded the tools on the bus and we drove away from the camp. We drove for about 10 or 15 minutes before the driver pulled over and told us to get off the bus. I saw that a big tree had fallen across the road and leaves and broken branches were all over the place. The C.O. told us that some of us would be responsible for clearing the fallen tree because the tree and its branches was blocking the road and clogging a stream that ran along the road. We were then divided into three work groups so while some of us were working on the tree the C.O. took the other two groups to work on other assignments around the island. My group unloaded some of the tools and got to work on the tree. After about three and a half hours the C.O. returned to pick us up. The other groups were already on the bus and we headed back to the camp where we went to the cafeteria to eat lunch. Over time I learned that in phase 1 we did do little maintenance and clean up jobs around the island but in phase 2 we would be given a job that we would work until we graduated from the program. After lunch we were taken into a classroom in the recreational building where we were given an orientation and overview of what to expect at the W.E.C.

A different C.O. introduced himself and began to run down the rules and camp schedule. We learned that on the weekdays we would P.T. for an hour before breakfast, we would work from 8am until 2pm, and then we would have educational classes from 3pm until 5:30 pm. Dinner was at 6 pm and after dinner we would be given free time until sobriety and life skills class from 8-9pm. From 9 pm until lights out at 10pm we were given free time where we were expected to prepare for the following day by showering and ironing our uniforms. We could place our dirty laundry in the laundry bags that we were given on the first day, turn it in at night and pick it up the evening of the next day.

On Saturdays and Sundays we were allowed more free time when we could play basketball or flag football. We didn't have to work on these days and we could receive visitors during established visiting times in the morning and early afternoon. I was excited about the visits because I had not seen my family since the day I turned myself in. Before turning myself in I decided that I didn't want Meko or my kids to visit me at the county jail because there was thick glass that separated me from them and I didn't want that kind of visit. While I was in the county jail after my initial arrest Meko brought Milan to visit me and Milan began to cry when she couldn't get to me. She was a few months old and didn't understand why she couldn't get through the glass between us. I didn't want that to happen again.

There were G.E.D. courses available to inmates who had not graduated from high school and higher learning classes where inmates could study for college credits. During our educational class period we worked in groups according to our educational capacity. This was determined by testing that was done the first week of our stay. I tested high and was placed in a group that took courses for college credit. We worked on English, math, and science and did some life skills work to determine what motivated our choices and decisions in order help us make better decisions in the future. Everyone was required to do the life skills work so we would often have sessions where a facilitator would talk to the group about our current situation to determine what may have led to our incarceration. These sessions were a bit tedious at times because I knew that drugs and a criminal lifestyle was the cause of my incarceration and I didn't want to spend a bunch of time rehashing the obvious, but over time I began to appreciate the reflection process that we used to look back over my life more carefully to locate critical moments in my development. Through some of these sessions I was able to better identify how my anger and frustration with my dad affected me and how his absence caused me to seek outside sources to cultivate my views on manhood. I also better understood how and why I didn't want to leave my children without a father. I began to think about how Milan cried while visiting me in the county jail when I couldn't hold her and I thought about Malia growing up without me in the house because K and I did not get along. I spent a lot of time meditating on my life situation and I decided that I never wanted to be incarcerated again. Not only was I frustrated by the loss of freedom and someone else determining where and when I could move around, what and when I could eat, and what clothing I must wear, but I was also tired of being around a bunch of cats who talked of nothing but how glorious their lives were while they were out on the streets. I quickly got tired of the war stories and the pimp chronicles and decided that I wanted to do something different and better with my life. I decided that I was going to use this opportunity to get strong and healthy mentally, physically, and spiritually and live a different life when I got out. I wrote several letters to Meko each week recording my growth and mental transformations and we made plans for a much brighter future. Little did I know that I still had not conquered my addiction and it would rear its ugly head again soon after my release.

My first month at the camp went pretty quickly. My mom and/or Meko came up to visit me on the weekends and kept me abreast of what was happening in the free world. They had to drive a half hour or so up to Tacoma to catch a ferry that brought them over to McNeil Island. They were then bussed over to the camp where we were housed. Meko came up about three times that first month bringing Malia, Milan, and my niece Tahdja with her. Tahdja was my sister Natasha's daughter and she was about a year and a half older than Milan. Tahdja and I were really close and I was just as glad to see her as Malia and Milan. Visits were held in the recreational building in the visitation area. There were vending machines where visitors could purchase food items to eat with the inmates during the visits and tables where families could sit. There were also toys for the children to play with and a fenced in outside area with picnic tables where families could sit on nice days. Visiting time was a three or four hour window and visitors could stay until visiting time ended. Visitors could buy $10 worth of food from the vending machines to send back to the room with the inmate after the visit and these items were very much appreciated in the evenings considering we were fed dinner at 5:30. After the visit we returned to our dorm after being searched to make sure we didn't receive any contraband. Visits were the highlight of the week and I eagerly looked forward to the weekend when I could see my family.

After two weeks of P.T. I was asked to lead P.T. for our phase. I was also told that there would be a P.T. competition that every phase competed in. This competition was a monthly event where the different phases performed calisthenics in cadence while performing different patterns and movements. Each phase performed a 5 minute routine and the C.O.s voted on the best performance and gave commissary items to the winning group. My phase won the competition in our first appearance. This was the first time a phase 1 group won the competition and a lot of people were surprised we won but no one could say we didn't have a great routine. Over the next three months we would win the competition again on each occasion going undefeated for the four months we were there. This was the first time this happened. I was asked to lead P.T. for all of the incoming phases for my entire time in the camp so I led the incoming phase 1 groups during the daily P.T. workouts and then I worked with my phase to prepare for the competitions.

The W.E.C. inmates weren't the only inmates at the camp; there were also a few general population inmates who worked in various areas around the campus. They worked in the kitchen and the laundry room and on road crews. In phase 1 we didn't have much contact with these inmates but the other phases worked right alongside them. In phase 2 I was assigned to a job on the road crew where I worked with four other general population inmates. I was assigned to the road crew because I had previous construction experience. During phase 1 we began to work on our resumes and job history so the C.O.s used this information to assign us to the jobs we would do for the remainder of our stay at W.E.C. As a road crew employee I was responsible for helping to maintain the grounds and roads around the island. I had a lot of freedom in this position and I learned numerous skills that would serve as job experience when I was released from prison. I learned to operate a backhoe, an excavator, and a vibrating press used to smooth asphalt on roads. I also learned how to operate a tractor with a mower attachment that was used to mow the grass alongside the roads on the island.

In the morning, after breakfast, I would pick up a sack lunch from the kitchen, board a van with the other road crew members, and ride over to the equipment lot where the heavy equipment was kept. We met inside the equipment building and received our daily assignments from the road crew foreman. Every day we were responsible for greasing and checking the equipment before we used it and noting any problems. Sometimes we worked together on large projects like road repair or lying or repairing sewer pipes, but other times I worked independently of the others and operated the lawn mower tractor. I enjoyed my road crew job and I was grateful for the opportunity to learn new skills that I would be able to use later.

One day at work I had a disagreement with one of the other inmates. We were in the equipment building and for some reason we got into an argument about how to do something. He was Caucasian and about 10 or 15 years older than me and he was on his second year of a four year bid. He began to call me derogatory names and act as if he was ready to fight. My first instinct was to strike him in the neck and break one of his arms or legs after he fell to the ground but before I acted I thought about how a fight would affect my placement at W.E.C. During orientation we were told that if we fought or we were caught with drugs or other contraband we would be put out of the program and forced to do our entire sentence. I was facing sixty three months for my offense if I got put out of the program so although it was difficult I controlled my anger and swallowed my pride. I didn't hit the man.

"You're lucky I'm in this program" I said, "Otherwise I would crush your punk a**." I told him.

I then walked outside to cool off and calm down. Another older African American dude came outside behind me and told me I had done the right thing. He said that sometimes general population inmates would instigate confrontations with W.E.C. inmates to get them kicked out of the program. This seemed a little scandalous but there were a lot of inmates who were upset that they didn't have the opportunity to shorten their sentences like we did. I thank God for allowing me to maintain my cool in that situation. I don't know how my family would have responded if I told them I got into a fight and instead of coming home after six months I had to do four and a half to five years. From that day on I kept an eye on the dude while I was working and maintained a safe distance so that I wouldn't be put in a situation where I had to do something that would jeopardize my program.

I continued to focus on the program and at the end of every month I received another stripe on the right sleeve of my shirt for a phase completion. Soon I had three stripes and I was in my final month. My last month seemed to drag on as our classes began to focus more on job placement and post incarceration activities. I received my finalized resume and I was given an address and a time to check in with my probation officer. I was also read a list of rules and expectations that if violated could cause me to be locked up again. A couple of days before my release our phase was given a going away celebration by the C.O.s. The Camp did this for every graduating phase prior to their departure so it felt good to have reached this point. On my final day I packed up all of my belongings and boarded the bus with my other phase members. We were taken to the ferry where we got off the bus and boarded the same ferry that brought our loved ones over to visit us on the weekends. As the ferry crossed the sound I remember how excited I was to be going home. It was the first week of June and I was out in time for Milan's first birthday. When we got to Tacoma and disembarked from the ferry my mom, Meko, and Milan were waiting for me. My mom jumped up and down in excitement as Meko smiled and Milan reached for me. I gave each of them a big hug and threw all of my stuff in the trunk of my mom's car. I was out of prison and back in society. I was happy and grateful. I had finished reading the bible during my time on McNeil Island and I was determined to do better with my life. Whereas in previous years I wasn't very concerned about doing time now I never again wanted to be locked up. I wanted to be there for my family and I wanted my freedom. I decided that I was going to try harder at doing the right thing and making good choices. Unfortunately, I had not acquired all of the tools I needed to maintain a healthy lifestyle so in time I would once again struggle with my vices.

Me at WEC

Me, Milan, & Tahdja at WEC

Meko & Milan visiting me at WEC

Milan, Me, & Meko 1995

Mom and I at WEC 1995

Chapter 6

DERELICT

I beseech ye therefore brethren, by the mercies of
God, that ye present your bodies a living sacrifice,
holy and acceptable unto God, which is your
reasonable service. And be not conformed to this
world: but be ye transformed by the renewing of
your mind, that you may prove that good, and
acceptable, and perfect, will of God.
Romans 12:1-2

In order to be released from prison we had to have a stable living environment arranged, so I gave them my mom's address in Federal Way. Meko and I talked about getting our own place but it was going to take me some time to get a job and get settled so my mom said I could stay with her until I could save some money. I only had a couple of months to stay with my mom because I found out that she planned to retire from Boeing in the next few weeks and move back to Mississippi to be closer to my grandmother. So I immediately began doing the things I needed to do to maintain my freedom. I checked in with my probation officer and set up a reporting schedule. Since my conviction was drug related I was required to give periodic urine samples and participate

165

in an outpatient drug rehabilitation program. This participation consisted of three meetings per week plus poof that I attended three Alcoholics Anonymous or Narcotics Anonymous meetings per week. I set all of these items in place and then began my job search. Surprisingly it wasn't very difficult for me to find a job. Even though I was recently released from prison I had a lot of warehouse and heavy equipment experience. I got a job as a deliveryman for another furniture company and I began to try to rebuild my life.

When I went to prison Meko was living with her grandmother and working for a phone company where she'd been employed for a number of years. While I was incarcerated she found a townhouse in Skyway and moved in with Milan. I worked for a couple of months and then moved in with Meko. Right after I moved in my mom moved to Mississippi with my nephew Alvedo, my sister Sheila's son. The Skyway townhouse was small but nice. On the ground floor there was a kitchen, dining room, and living room. Upstairs there was a lofted bedroom and a bathroom. The bedroom had a low wall that overlooked the downstairs so you could see the living room and dining room. I was happy to be with my family working and doing the right thing.

A few months after my release I decided to go hang out with some of my friends. This was a violation of my probation which stipulated that I remain alcohol and drug free and stay away from any known felons. Most of my friends were felons as a result of the war on drugs and unless I removed myself from the city entirely it was difficult for me to stay away from the friends I grew up with. My friends and I went to a club downtown where we acted up until the club closed. I had a few drinks and for some reason decided that I was going to go get high. It had been almost a year since I had ingested any type of intoxicating substance but after the few drinks I began to again think about taking a hit of crack cocaine. I had my friend drop me off at a bar on Madison where I used to hang out and I easily found some rock and a place to sit and smoke. After the first hit I felt bad about being back in this environment and risking my freedom but I was unable to stop taking hits. I figured I would finish what I had and then have a few drinks to calm me down before going home. Unfortunately before I knew it several hours had passed and it was four o-clock in the morning. I spent all of my money and I didn't have any beer or liquor to calm my high down. I didn't want to smoke any weed because I knew that weed stayed in your system for up to thirty days and I didn't want to get a dirty Urine Analysis on my next probation appointment. I wasn't as worried about the alcohol and crack because I knew the alcohol would be gone in hours and crack cleared your system in a few days.

I left the house where I was smoking and started walking down 22nd street south toward Union. When I got to Union I walked up to 21st to see if anyone I knew was out there. It was about 4:30am so the streets were pretty bare except for a few people hanging out drinking or smoking in dark corners. I was thinking about how to get some more money and more dope when a dude walked up to me and asked me if I knew where he could get some work. He was a short stocky black dude wearing shorts and a t-shirt and carrying a bag with two twenty two ounce bottles of beer. I looked at him closely to determine if he was a police officer and then asked him,

"Are you the police?"

"Hell no" he said.

I figured he wouldn't be a police officer out by himself at 4:30 in the morning but I decided to take some precautions just in case. I hadn't seen anyone selling since I got there but I didn't let him know this.

Just like that I forgot the time I spent away from my family while incarcerated and my plans to remain free by avoiding the mistakes I'd made in the past. The drugs and alcohol in my system prevented me from making sound and logical decisions and I fell back into an old pattern.

"How much you want?" I asked.

"Thirty," He replied.

"Come on" I said.

We walked south toward Cherry Street to a house where I knew people would be selling or smoking dope. We walked the four or five blocks and I made small talk to help the dude relax so he didn't think I was trying to get over on him. When we got to the house I told him to give me the money because the people didn't know him and we could get a better deal if I was spending the money. He gave me the money and I knocked on the door.

A cat I knew answered the door and I asked him who had some work. He let us in and told us to sit at a kitchen table. We sat at the table and the dude I was with opened one of the beers he brought and took a sip. The cat that let us in went upstairs for a moment before coming back down with about a $20 rock. I told him that he would have to do better than that but the other dude wanted it. Since I had the money I told him to be patient. The dude that brought it down continued to try to convince us by telling us it was the bomb and we could try it before buying it if we wanted to. He put a piece on a pipe and let the dude with me take a hit. He then put another piece on and I took a hit. It was good dope but I told him he would have to do better than that for $30.

Suddenly the dude I was with hit me in the head with one of the 22 ounce beer bottles, he wanted the dope on the table and he didn't want to wait for a better deal.

"Give me my money," he said as I stumbled to my feet.

The bottle broke over my head and beer was running down my face into my eyes. I still had the money in my right hand so I reached out to grab him with my left hand while I punched him in the head with my balled up right hand. He grabbed the second unopened bottle and hit me over the head with that one as well. I wasn't really as fazed by the blow as he thought I would be and he seemed surprised when I charged him and slammed him against the wall. We tussled against the wall for a moment and then I felt my feet slipping in the beer on the kitchen floor. I was unable to get any leverage and slipped to one knee, pulling him down with me. We continued to tussle on the floor and somehow made our way into the living room. I must admit the dude was pretty strong so it was hard to get him in a hold where I could gain an advantage. I got better footing on the carpet in the living room and slammed him on the couch and began to throw blows to his head. I still couldn't really see because of the beer in my eyes but I had a pretty good idea where he was. He was punching me back and connected on a couple of blows. We were fighting oblivious to the homeowners when I felt someone grab me from behind. I was yanked off of the dude and lost my balance. I tripped over the coffee table behind me and fell on my back. The dude took advantage of this opportunity and jumped on top of me as I fell to the floor.

Now I was in a bad position. I tried to lift him off of me as he tried to maintain his position while throwing punches at my head and chest. I reached out with my left hand and tried to poke him in the eye and then roll out from under him. This move had worked for me when a big dude jumped me and tried to rob me in downtown Seattle. In that incident I was able to get my thumb into the dude's eye and he fell back enough for me to get out of a dangerous situation. Unfortunately, it didn't work this time. He pulled back out of my reach. With a burst of strength I arched my back and threw him off of me and jumped to my feet while he tried to regain his composure. We faced off again when I guess he decided that it wasn't worth the fight. I watched him walk out the door and I was about to step out on the porch to make sure he was leaving when I heard police sirens and saw a police car pull up to the front of the house.

The dude told the police that I took his money. They didn't believe me when I denied it so I was arrested. They took me to the hospital first because I had some cuts from the bottles hitting me in the head. After stitching me up I was booked into King county jail. I still had the $30 but they found it when they searched me for drugs and weapons. I was booked into jail where I stayed for the weekend. After my arraignment on Monday I was released on my own recognizance and I headed home.

I went back to work the following day and resumed my daily routine. I was upset that I put myself in that position and I vowed to myself that I would try harder to stay focused on doing what I was supposed to do.

About three or four days later I was at work, returning to the warehouse in the truck after delivering some furniture, when I noticed two Tukwila police cars parked in the lot. I backed the truck up to the loading dock and went into the warehouse expecting to clean out my truck, finish my work day, and go home. I knew something was up when I was called in to the warehouse office where my probation officer was waiting for me.

The report of my arrest for fighting had gotten to his desk so he was there with the police to arrest me for a probation violation. They cuffed me and put me in the back of the police car as my coworkers watched and talked about me amongst themselves. I was booked into King County jail on a no bail warrant and sent back to the eighth floor. I ended up losing my job as a result of the arrest and I spent several weeks in jail waiting on my court dates for the fight. It was the fall of 1995 and I remember watching the Million Man March on television as I sat in a jail cell. I remember thinking that I should be there instead of in here and I knew that if I had tried to go to the march my family would have supported me wholeheartedly. About a week later I was released when the dude I was fighting failed to show up for court. I was through with incarceration and I walked out of jail for what would be my last time.

When I got out of jail I went home to our apartment in Skyway. I found a new job as a forklift operator but my home life became stressed when I began to hang out with the wrong crowd again. I got into a car accident while riding with a friend after getting high all night. My friend later shot himself in the head while playing with his gun. Meko and I began to argue more because of my bad choices and her fear that I would end up back in prison or dead on the streets from smoking crack. She began to hang out more with her friends and take little trips out of town on girls' weekends. I knew I didn't want to lose Meko or end up back in prison behind drugs so I worked with my addiction prevention program and arranged another 90 day stay at Cedar Hills.

This time around I was more focused on staying sober and getting as many tools as I possibly could to assist me. While in treatment I realized that most of the friends that I'd grown up with were living lifestyles that were detrimental to my sobriety. I came to understand that if I wanted to stay sober I would need to change my environment and the people I hung out with.

When I got out of treatment I went to stay with my dad in Marysville, Washington. Marysville is a small rural town about 60 miles north of Seattle. My dad owned a house there where he lived with his girlfriend Barb and their son, my younger brother, Terrance. Barb also had two other boys from a previous relationship named Jeff and Donnie who lived with them. My dad said it was ok for me to stay with them for a while to get myself together so I moved to Marysville.

I looked around for a job and was hired at a lumber mill about five miles north of my dad's house. I woke up at 6 in the morning and rode my bike 20 minutes to work every weekday morning. I worked for 8 hours and then I rode my bike home. I was paid about $12 per hour which was pretty good money but this was the hardest job that I ever worked. We stacked and moved stacks of boards all day, only stopping for a half hour lunch and two fifteen minute breaks. The board stacks were heavy and awkward so by the end of the day I was sore from the repetition of the movements. I lasted about three months at this job before I decided to find something else to do. I was hired as a delivery driver for a salsa company and found that this new job was more to my liking. I was responsible for assisting in the production of salsa products for a small family owned company and then delivering the finished product to retail stores around Washington state. I liked this job better so I was able to hang on to this position for a while.

Before I knew it I had almost nine months free from crack. I was feeling pretty good and returning to myself. Meko and I would see each other periodically but we were on a bit of a break while I tried to get myself together. She moved back in with her grandmother after I left so I would go to visit her there every once in a while or she would bring Milan out to see me at my dad's house. I was doing pretty well at my dad's house. I had a few new friends who I hung out with and I was even taking a few classes at Everett Community College.

In September of 1996 I was riding with my dad listening to the radio when the announcer reported that Tupac had been shot in Las Vegas. When we got home I called Meko, who was in Vegas with her friends, to find out if she knew anything about the shooting. Even though she and her girlfriends were a few blocks down the strip from where the shooting took place they were unaware that it happened because of all of the activity and the crowd that was there for the Mike Tyson fight. A couple of days later it was announced that Tupac Shakur died. I went to my room and sat on my weight bench and cried. I was surprised by how sad I was that this rapper was killed, but I realized that he was much more than a rapper to me. I totally identified with his lyrics and much of what he spoke of resonated with me. I believe that Tupac was a prophet and if he had lived and turned the corner in his personal spiritual development he would have become a voice that could have moved my generation like the voice of Martin Luther King moved a generation in the 60's. Unfortunately, he was taken before his leadership qualities could be developed for society's welfare.

Later that month I came in to Seattle for my cousin Chelsea's wedding. Chelsea went straight to Howard University after grad-uating from Garfield and then moved to the east coast to pursue her career. She met some dude over there who asked her to marry him and she said yes, so now they were getting married. I had not met her fiancé so I was eager to meet him. Chelsea was like a sister to me so I wanted to be sure the guy she was marrying was going to be good to her. My brother and I had to rough up one or two of her boyfriends when we were growing up and I still felt a responsibility to look out for her.

I'd heard through the family grapevine that Chelsea's fiancé was a white Jewish dude so there was a lot of anticipation when it came to meeting him. When I finally did meet Jamie I liked him almost immediately. He seemed cool and most importantly Chelsea seemed very happy with him. I first met Jamie at my aunt Tee's house when he and Chelsea came to Seattle to prepare for the wedding. He and Chelsea were staying with Tee and I must admit it was a little weird to see him come out of the bathroom in his pajamas. After talking to Jamie I found out that he was from Boston and his dad was a famous announcer for the Celtics. I told him that Chelsea was like a sister to me and it was very important that he take good care of her. He said he understood my concern but he loved her dearly and he planned to make her very happy. We shook hands and then I gave him a big bear hug that squeezed the air out of him and that was that. Chelsea and Jamie had a beautiful wedding at Mount Zion and then we all went to a mansion they rented for the reception. Chelsea threw her bouquet and Meko caught it which caused me to get more than a little teasing from my family members. My brother Doobie and my cousin Neil snuck away with a box of liquor and we went to the hotel where all of Chelsea's bridesmaids were staying to hang out. It was a great day and all of our family was there including my grandmother, my mom, and Alvedo who came up from Mississippi. We partied into the evening celebrating this joyous occasion not knowing that the next time our family came together it would be to mourn.

About a month later, on Sunday October 20th, Meko and I were at Meko's grandmother's house when my sister Sheila called me to tell me that my mom had been rushed to a hospital in Mississippi.

My mom retired from Boeing and moved to Mississippi with my nephew Alvedo in the summer of 1995. I believe she was tired of the rat race in Seattle and wanted to be closer to her mother who never left Mississippi. After years at Boeing my mom decided that she wanted to do something different and when the Boeing Company offered the staff a termination package as part of a period of downsizing she took it. In Mississippi she went in a totally different direction becoming a nail technician. She was very happy doing manicures and pedicures and talking to the women who came into the shop where she worked.

My nephew told me that on the day my mom was rushed to the hospital they were at home when suddenly he heard her yell out in pain from another room. When he rushed into the room he found her holding her head while complaining of severe pain. He called the ambulance that immediately came and transported her to the hospital.

When I got the call, and found out that my mom was in the hospital unconscious, my first thought was, 'I need to get there.' I called my dad in Marysville and told him what happened. Meko and I drove out there to get money for a bus ticket and I hopped on the first bus I could get headed to Mississippi.

I prayed a lot on my way to Mississippi. I truly believed that if I could get there in time my mom would be ok. At every stop I got off the bus and called Meko who was in Seattle monitoring the situation by staying in contact with my relatives in Mississippi. I kept a journal of my thoughts and prayers as I traveled across country and spent a lot of time reflecting on life. On Tuesday night I couldn't sleep and I was looking out the window at a clear sky as we traveled through some countryside. The lights inside the bus were off so I could see the stars in the sky quite well. As I gazed up into the sky I thought I saw my mom's face in the sky. I stared for a number of minutes and I was almost sure it was her face. After a moment she winked at me and disappeared. I grabbed my journal and wrote down what I'd seen and then I sat for a long time wondering what it meant. I called Meko and asked how my mom was doing and she told me that she was in the same condition as the day before. She told me that my mom suffered from a brain aneurism that burst and she was unconscious while the doctors tried to treat the problem.

I arrived in Jackson on Thursday morning, after three days on the bus, and was picked up by one of my cousins who lived in Jackson. Although I was the first to leave Seattle I would be the last to arrive in Mississippi. It turns out that my cousin Melanie was able to find affordable last minute airline tickets so when I arrived I found out that Meko and most of my extended family was already there.

"Take me to the hospital so I can see my mom," I said as I grabbed my luggage and loaded it into my cousin's car.

"Your mom's not at the hospital," she said.

"What do you mean? Where is she," I asked confused. On every call I made I was told that she was in the hospital and I called just hours before arriving in Jackson.

"Where's my mom?" I asked.

Tears began to well up in my cousin's eyes.

"Your mom passed away on Tuesday," she said.

"What," I said, "no, they just told me she was in the hospital."

My family didn't want me to hear about my mom's death while I was on the bus so they waited until I arrived to tell me. They didn't want me alone when I found out because they didn't want me to do something dangerous or destructive out of anger and sorrow. My cousin took me straight to the funeral home where I saw my mom in a casket. I immediately broke down in a fit of angry sadness.

There was a time when I felt that the only thing that I couldn't bear was the loss of my mom and now here I was faced with that very thing. My whole life my mom had been there for me. She was there screaming for me at my football games, baseball games, and track meets and supporting me in everything that I did. She housed me and loved me in spite of my stupidity and ignorance and through addiction and incarceration she was there for me. My mom never turned her back on me and she was the one person I knew who loved me unconditionally.

Words cannot express how I felt.

My mom! My mom! My mom! My mom!

My mom was gone. What the f***!!!

My cousin took me to meet the rest of my family in my grandmother's hometown and I found out that my uncle Earnest and my grandmother decided to disconnect my mom from life support when the doctors told them that she wouldn't recover. For a while I was upset with my uncle and grandmother but after a day or so I realized that my grandmother probably knew best and if she thought that letting my mom go was the best thing to do than it probably was. I had hoped to see my mom again and I was heartbroken because I got there too late to help her. My heart was truly broken and I knew life would never be the same.

All of my family from Seattle was there so we started planning the homegoing service. In a sense I began the process of becoming a man in those two weeks I stayed in Mississippi planning my mother's funeral service and celebrating her life. I began to think about my responsibility not just to my children but to all of my family. I had a new perspective on a lot of things. My brother Doobie had once found me smoking crack in the street and said to me, "You're making yourself look bad, you're making us look bad." I didn't understand what he meant at the time but now I was beginning to see how intricately our family was connected and what it meant to lose one member to addiction, incarceration, or death. I better understood that in life everyone is affected directly or indirectly by the actions of others.

My mom's funeral service was very difficult. There were a lot of kind words spoken about my mom and gallons of tears cried by all of us who would miss one of the best people God ever created. My grandmother began to wail when we walked by the open casket at the close of the service and as I held her to comfort her and keep her from hurting herself I remember being surprised by how strong and solid she was.

We made it through the funeral and we went back to my grandmother's house to eat, sing, dance, mourn, cry, and celebrate my mom's life. I stayed for a few more days to help close out all of my mom's business and then Alvedo and I jumped on a train that would take us back to Seattle. Meko and most of my family members had already left so my uncle Earnest took Alvedo and I to the train station in Jackson. It took us a few days to get to Seattle but when we arrived I went back to my dad's house in Marysville and Alvedo went to stay with Tee.

At my dad's house the dynamic had changed. I no longer felt like a child even though in a sense I was in a child's place living under my dad's roof. I was 28 years old living with my dad and I realized that something was wrong. I had gone from living with my mom in Federal Way to living with my dad when she moved to Mississippi. My dad and I began to clash almost immediately after my return from Mississippi. It was like when a young lion grows up in a pride under the rule of an elder lion. The elder lion is used to eating first. Once the younger lion is big enough to think that he should eat first it's time for him to go. I was ready to eat first now so it was time for me to go and establish my own territory. My dad and I got into an argument one day when he walked into my bedroom without knocking on the door and I knew it was time to go.

"This is my house," he said when I complained about him not knocking.

"You're right," I said, "This is your house."

I immediately got up and packed my clothing into two large suitcases and left. I didn't have a car and I didn't want to ask my dad for a ride so I walked two miles to the bus stop carrying the two huge pieces of luggage. I caught a bus in to Seattle and placed my luggage in a locker at the Greyhound station. My head was spinning. I didn't know what to do. I was angry at my dad and I was still hurt by my mom's passing and now I didn't know where I was going to stay. Meko had returned to school and rented a two bedroom apartment on campus but I really didn't want to go stay with her. I didn't know what to do so I decided to go get high.

I went downtown and bought some rock and found a few cats I knew and hung out smoking for the next few days. When I came to my senses I went to Meko's apartment where she welcomed me in and allowed me to stay. I only went on a few binges over the next couple of months. I found a job at Office Depot near the apartment and started going to worship services at a church in the central district. But I was still struggling. One night I was awakened by a very vivid dream. In my heart I felt like God was telling me that I needed to stop going back and forth. Somehow, I knew that I could never overcome my struggles with addiction until I committed myself to God totally and stopped going back and forth between the street life and a family life. Something told me that it wasn't right for me to be living with Meko outside of wedlock and that I needed to leave. I told Meko how I felt and she said she understood. We decided to give our relationship a break to see if it was God's will for us to be together. It was about 11:30pm and she felt that I would probably be able to find somewhere to stay the next day, but I felt that the need to leave was more immediate. So I got a blanket and a pillow and I went across the street to a park and slept on a bench. The next morning I took the pillow and blanket back to Meko and told her I was going to go stay in a shelter until I could figure something else out. I didn't want to be a burden to anyone else and I felt that God was testing me in a way to find out what I was willing to give up to be obedient to Him.

That night I stayed at the Union Gospel Mission in downtown Seattle. For a week I was in line at 6pm for dinner, a church service, and a spot on the floor in the chapel. The second week I joined a discipleship program on the second floor and got a more permanent bed space that only participants in the program were offered. The program participants had jobs around the mission and helped facilitate the meals, the chapel services, and other duties around the mission. We were expected to wear business casual clothing so we were given an opportunity to pick out clothing from a room where donated clothing was accumulated. We also had access to a weight room in the basement of the building. We attended bible study classes every day and we were required to memorize a certain number of scriptures before we moved up to the next level of the discipleship program. After a month in the program I'd memorized enough verses to move to a ranking that allowed me to work outside the mission. I began to work with my uncle Edgar who was a trained electrician. Uncle Edgar was my mom's oldest brother. He was the first of her siblings to move to Seattle and he helped the rest of his brothers and sisters move to the city. Eventually I moved out of the Union Gospel Mission and stayed in a church shelter where there were only about ten men who slept in the church gym. We alternated meal cooking responsibilities and were free to work and do our own thing during the day as long as we remained sober and got permission to stay away from the church overnight. At some point I talked to my cousin Chelsea, who was now living with her husband Jamie in New York City, and learned that there was an opportunity for me to come to New York and work in the film and video industry. This was like a dream come true. New York City! I worked with my uncle for another month to save some money and then in the summer of 97 I bought a one way ticket to New York.

I packed a couple of suitcases, said goodbye to my family, and hopped on the plane with excitement and anticipation. Meko took me to the airport and I kissed her and Milan before boarding the plane. This was in 1997, before the planes crashed into the World Trade Center, so you could walk departing passengers all the way to their gates of departure. Meko and I talked about marriage, and we were doing better as a result of my recent sobriety, but Meko was unsure whether she wanted to put up with my sporadic and unpredictable drug use. We still loved one another so we agreed to see how this trip went before deciding how to move forward.

I landed at LaGuardia Airport and took a cab into the city. Chelsea met me at Port Authority and we took a jitney cab through the Lincoln tunnel over to the Jersey side of the Hudson River. Chelsea and Jamie lived in a little one bedroom apartment in West New York, New Jersey about a block from the river. Chelsea was working as a production coordinator for a major television company and Jamie was a successful video director. They both worked in the film and video industry so they were able to help me get my foot in the door and start working as a freelance production assistant or a P.A. Production assistant work was fun and exciting. On any given day I would be responsible for duties that varied from picking up equipment, talent, and food to locking down shoot locations so that onlookers didn't disrupt the shoot. As a freelance P.A. I was not guaranteed work so I had to develop relationships with a number of producers and production coordinators to ensure that when one producer wasn't working on a project I could work with someone else who had something going on.

I loved living in New York. I would wake up and take the jitney cab into the city and get off at the Port Authority and then walk around Times Square or take the subway to other parts of the city. One day I took the subway up to 125th street and got off so I could walk around and see Harlem. I was walking down 125th street looking at the shops and taking in the sights when suddenly somebody grabbed me by the arm.

"Marty, what's up?"

It was a cat named Pug from Seattle.

"What's up Pug?" I said, surprised to see a Seattle cat in New York. "What are you doing here?"

Pug told me that he came to New York with a few other dudes I knew and a couple of girls just to kick it. We went over to one of the shops and the Seattle cats were in there shopping. I said "what's up" and we gave daps all around. I hung out with these guys for a couple of days driving around the city and going to a few parties but eventually I had to go back to work. These cats were balling and I couldn't keep up with their spending. I remember one of them spending $1,000.00 on a pair of pants and a Versace shirt before a party. Even in my most prosperous days I couldn't see myself spending $1,000.00 on one outfit. So I cut out and headed back to West New York.

As I traveled through the city I remember listening to Usher's song, 'You Make Me Wanna,' and thinking that this was how I felt about Seattle and New York. I was ready to leave Seattle and start a new relationship with a new spot. I was feeling good and things were going well. Chelsea and Jamie were nice enough to let me stay with them for a few months so I could save enough money to get my own spot. I paid them a few hundred dollars every month but they put it into an account and when I moved out they gave it back to me so I could use it to get established in my new spot. I really appreciated them opening their home to me and helping me the way they did.

After a few months in New York I found a little boarding house in Crown Heights and I rented a room. The house was really a single family dwelling but the owner rented out rooms in the basement for $100 a week. There were three rooms in the basement and the other two rooms were occupied when I moved in. We shared a bathroom and a kitchen and a separate entrance. The room next to me housed a woman about my age and her daughter who was about 8 or 9 years old. The other room was occupied by a dude who I never saw the entire time I lived there. My room was small but furnished with a television, a bedroom set that included a full sized bed, a dresser, and two nightstands. I settled in to my spot and continued working thinking that I could upgrade over time.

Crown Heights was an interesting area. I remember seeing Hasidic Jews for the first time and being fascinated by the diversity of cultures in the neighborhood. I went to the West Indian Day Parade and was overwhelmed by the floats and the crowds as they traveled up Eastern Parkway. I stood and looked down the Parkway and as far as I could see there where hundreds of thousands of people lining the streets as floats carrying celebrities blared music and slowly crawled along. It was like Carnival in Brazil with women dancing around in elaborate costumes with flowing feathers and huge wings. I bought some jerk chicken from a Jamaican lady who was selling meals from a grill that she set up in front of her house and I was blown away by how delicious it was.

There was nothing like this in my experience in Seattle and I yearned to see more of what the world had to offer. I went to Washington DC with Chelsea for Howard University's homecoming and since I missed the Million Man March I decided to accompany Chelsea and a bunch of her college friends to the Million Woman March that was held in Philadelphia. Life was good.

I continued doing P.A. work and had the opportunity to work with several celebrities during that period. I did a lot of production work with MTV and other Viacom channels as well as commercial work with companies like Burger King and KFC. I worked on a couple of movies and made several contacts in the film industry. I was doing pretty well and I hoped that Meko might consider moving to New York with me.

Meko and I were talking on the phone often but Meko didn't really want to be in a relationship with me anymore, she was tired of the inconsistency. I, on the other hand, did not want to end the relationship. I loved Meko but I also wanted to be a father who was present in Milan's life. I saw how difficult life was for Malia after her mother and I broke up and I didn't want to see that happen to Milan as well. Hoping to work on our relationship I booked a flight to Seattle so I could be with my family on Christmas.

In Seattle I found that many of my friends were still in the game. I had several months of sobriety but before I knew it I was back in crack house. I hung out for a couple of days and then separated myself from the hood and went to stay with Meko. I stayed sober for the rest of my stay and then boarded a plane back to New York. When I got back to New York I found that my taste for dope had been restored and I began to crave crack again. Every few days I would cut through the hood and cop a few nickel bags on the way home from work. I maintained my work, however, and avoided hanging out in the streets. After all, these were not streets that I was familiar with and I was wise enough to know that the drug game was twice as deadly in unfamiliar territory.

I eventually moved in with a female friend from Seattle who lived in the Park Slope section of Brooklyn. We were just friends and she had a boyfriend but we figured I could help her out with rent instead of paying for the tiny room I was occupying in Crown Heights. I moved in and agreed to pay about $300 per month for rent. About a week after moving in Meko, my sister Tash, and two of their girlfriends came to New York for the NBA All Star weekend. After work I met up with them at their hotel and we rode the subway into Brooklyn where a friend of ours from Seattle was having a party. I left them there while I went home and changed clothes and then went back to get them. We left Brooklyn and went in to the city to attend a party another Seattle cat was throwing at a club. In spite of my attempts to reconcile our relationship Meko still wasn't ready to reconnect so we remained broken up. Meko and her crew left after the weekend and I returned to work.

By this time I was smoking crack more often and since I did not want to do it in the apartment I shared with my roommate I began to hang out in the streets near Port Authority. One evening I came home after a few days in the street and went to bed. My roommate had a sofa bed in the living room where I slept. When I awoke Chelsea, Jamie, my roommate, and her boyfriend were standing around me looking at me with concern. It turns out that I began to toss and turn and cry out in my sleep like I'd done in the past and this scared my roommate so much that she called her boyfriend and my cousin to come over to see what was wrong with me. My roommate wasn't the only person who I'd scared while I struggled with demons in my sleep. On a previous occasion I woke up at

Meko's apartment in Seattle surrounded by police and firefighters. Meko had called 911 while I slept and the police officers came with the firefighters who woke me up and examined me before leaving. We decided that I should return to Seattle and the next day Chelsea and Jamie put me on a plane. I knew that it was a good idea to head back to Seattle because I was losing my focus and although I was still working I was smoking more. I landed in Seattle and caught a cab to my sister Sheila's house in Kent. I stayed with my sister Tash for a couple of months until I found a job and then I moved into a boarding house in the University district. Meko and I were still broken up so I didn't talk to her for a number of weeks after my return. I got a job at a glass company where a childhood friend was a manager and I started rebuilding. I returned to Mount Calvary Christian Center where I was going to church before moving to New York and I tried to once again focus on staying sober and getting my life together. I bought a little car and put some beats in it and I spent quality time with my children. I didn't like being back in Seattle but I knew I still had work to do on myself. I didn't know why I kept resorting to drug use but I believed it had something to do with my resistance to turning my life over to God 100%. I knew that God loved me and wanted me to serve Him but I was afraid of what that meant. I was worried about what I would have to give up in order to serve God wholeheartedly. In spite of this I believe God kept me even while I was in the streets. I would thank Him for watching over me and keeping me safe and I would ask Him to forgive me my sins every time I passed a church. Whether on foot or in a car, I would recite a prayer because I truly believed that God was there for me and one day I would be able to walk away from drug addiction for good.

One day after months of sobriety I decided to get high. I went on a drug run and stayed in the streets for several days. I eventually lost my job when I missed work because I was out getting high. I ended up on a 30 day run where I sold the speakers and sound system out of my car and then eventually I sold the car. I got my last paycheck and bought a few clothes, rented a hotel room, and spent the rest on dope. After 30 days in the streets I weighed 150 pounds and my clothing was hanging off of my thin frame. When all of the money was gone I returned to my boarding house room and sat in the dark trying to resist the urge to go out and commit a crime to get more crack. At some point I broke down and began to pray asking God to help me resist the temptation to go back in the streets and begging Him for a way out of this life. It was Friday night so I went to sleep and tried to get the thoughts of dope out of my head. The next day I woke up around 1pm and went down to the common area to watch television. I was hungry but I didn't have any money so I just sat in the dark watching TV and fighting the temptation to go out and start hustling for some money.

About 4pm Meko came to the boarding house looking for me. I had not spoken to her in a month and she told me she thought I was dead. She began to cry when she saw how thin I was and I could tell that she loved me and was genuinely concerned about me. She asked me if I was hungry, to which I replied yes, and we got in her car and went to get something to eat. On our way back to my room she asked me if I wanted to go to church in the morning. Initially I had reservations because I was ashamed and I didn't want anyone to see me looking all thin and smoked out but I told her that if she picked me up in the morning I would go. I'd prayed for God to help me resist the temptation to go back in the streets and He sent Meko to feed me and give me a way out. They say that if you take one step to God he will take two towards you. I didn't know how true that was but I knew that I couldn't do this thing on my own and I hated the person I'd become. I didn't want to live like this any longer and I was willing give God what He desired of me. I'd reached my bottom and I needed God to pick me up

Grandma & Milan 1996

Me, Malik, Sheila, Doobie, & Tash 1996

Chapter 7

REDEMPTION

The Spirit of the Lord is upon me, for He has
anointed me to preach the gospel to the poor; He
has sent me to heal the brokenhearted, to preach
deliverance to the captives, and recovery of sight
to the blind, to set at liberty them that are bruised.
To preach the acceptable year of the Lord.
Luke 4:18-19

Meko picked me up on Sunday morning and we headed over to Mt. Calvary. Meko and I had not joined Mt. Calvary but we went periodically together and it was now the main church that I attended. Mt. Calvary was associated with the Church of God in Christ and it was founded and pastored by Reggie C. Witherspoon who grew up in the central area of Seattle. His wife was Sister Laura and they both had large families in the Seattle area. I was attracted to Mt. Calvary because of Pastor Witherspoon's focus on helping men understand what it meant to be a man of God and therefore a real man. Around the time I started attending there was an influx of men around my age who were joining the church after leaving lives of drug dealing, gang violence, pimping, and other street lifestyles. I knew many of the young men who were joining from their street activities and I was moved to see them in church praising God after turning their lives around. On one occasion two former drug dealers came in and laid several guns on the altar at Pastor Witherspoon's feet as they gave up their prior lifestyle and surrendered to what God was doing in their lives.

On the Sunday that Meko and I went the church was packed as usual and the choir was jamming. I was sitting on the right side near the rear of the church listening to the sermon and feeling uncomfortable because of how I looked when suddenly something the pastor said resonated with me. I can't recall exactly what the sermon was about but at the end of the sermon Pastor Witherspoon came down from the altar and began praying for people. He made his way back to where Meko and I were standing along with the rest of the congregation and told me that God wanted to use me to do something great. He then placed his hands on my head and began to pray while the rest of the church extended their hands towards me and prayed as well. I was around the church enough to see people slain in the Spirit as the Holy Spirit descended upon them causing them to fall out or act out in unpredictable ways. This, however, didn't happen to me. I didn't fall out but I did fall back into my chair where I began crying and praying in the Spirit. I sat in my chair deep in prayer and oblivious to what was going on around me for a long time and when I was able to stand again a sense of power and peace engulfed me. I immediately began to praise God and thank Him for what He had done in my life. I cannot describe how I felt but for some reason I knew that I was no longer bound by addiction. I left the church that day feeling better than I could ever remember feeling. I didn't know what was ahead of me but I was no longer fearful. I trusted God to lead me and provide for me.

Meko and I went to get something to eat and then she took me back to my boarding house. Before she left she agreed to pick me up the next day so I could go look for a job. I went into my room and fell to my knees and prayed, cried, and worshiped God for a long time before getting up and going to the common room to watch TV. I no longer felt tempted to go out into the streets and I wasn't worried about what I was going to do next. I didn't know what God had in store for me but I was sure that my life had changed for the better.

The next day Meko picked me up and we went downtown so that I could fill out some job applications. We walked around to different places of business for a few hours and ended up on 2nd and Virginia around 11:30. I noticed a restaurant called Farestart and saw a sandwich board out front that advertised an all you can eat lunch buffet for six or seven dollars. Meko and I only had about $8 between us so I asked the hostess if it would be possible for Meko and I to share a meal. The hostess was a very nice African American woman maybe 5 or 10 years older than me. She looked at us and then told me.

"I can't do that, but if you pay for one meal I'll pay for the other."

Meko and I paid for one meal and thanked her for her kindness. We then grabbed some plates, filled them with food at the buffet, and sat down to eat. While we were eating I looked around the restaurant and noticed that the servers didn't look like regular servers. They appeared to be in training with a manager who was giving instruction on how to do various tasks. When I was able to get the hostess' attention I asked her what kind of restaurant this was. She told me that it was actually a four month program where homeless and disenfranchised men and women were trained in the culinary arts and helped to find jobs. She told me that she went through the program and she was now the head hostess of the restaurant. I learned that not only did the program provide culinary arts training but they also provided addiction recovery and life skills classes while providing housing for the participants. It was Monday and she told me that they would be holding orientation the very next day. I looked at Meko and thanked God for having brought us to exactly where I needed to be.

I returned the next day for orientation and learned all about the Farestart program.

Farestart was a Seattle based non-profit that gave homeless and marginalized individuals training in the culinary arts and helped them find employment at the completion of the four month training program. Along with the job training students took life skills classes and received assistance in interviewing techniques and resume preparation. There were also addiction recovery classes and referrals for individuals who required mental health evaluations and assistance. The program provided housing for the students for the duration of their involvement and assisted graduating students in finding housing once they completed the program.

This program was a Godsend for me. I went to orientation on Tuesday and by Thursday afternoon there was a bed available for me at a shelter in Pioneer Square called the Compass Center. I moved into the Compass Center on Thursday and began the program on the following Monday morning.

The first month in the program consisted of training and classes five days a week. We were off on Saturdays and Sundays so we could do whatever we wanted on those days. I became more involved at Mt. Calvary and attended worship services every Sunday morning and bible studies on Wednesday evenings. I also began to carry my bible with me everywhere I went so that I could read it whenever I had some free time. I remember being fascinated by one of the minsters at Mt. Calvary who seemed to have such a mastery of the biblical texts that she was able to quote scriptures almost effortlessly. Her name was Sister Pavi and when she got up to pray or minister I was always moved by her genuine love for God and the commitment she showed to God's word. I decided that in order for me to live a life that was pleasing to God I would need to learn the Word of God so that I could apply it in the situations of life that I was facing. So I devoted hours daily to prayer and the study of the biblical text.

I really enjoyed cooking so at Farestart I focused on excelling in my training. I learned a lot about commercial cooking that I had previously known very little about. We learned about proper cooking temperatures for various food items and proper food storage techniques. We were tested on these lessons and received our food handling cards. We learned knife skills and how to identify and use different herbs and spices. We learned to how make sauces and filet fish. We also learned how to identify the different cuts of meat on a cow. The training at Farestart did an excellent job of preparing us students for a job in the restaurant industry. However, not everyone in the program was focused on bettering their situation. There were some people in the program who only wanted the free perks that the program had to offer. On one occasion somebody called me a teacher's pet because I always sat in the front of the class and took notes on the lessons.

"I already know how to bang, sell crack, smoke crack, and go to jail," I told him. "I'm trying to learn how to stay free, invest in stocks and bonds, own a house and a business, take care of my family, and live."

I wasn't interested in the war stories or conversations about new ways to get over. I was on a mission to change my life like never before and I was taking full advantage of the opportunity that God blessed me with. Hope was restored where I had at one time felt hopeless. I began to like myself again and I wanted to be the best me that I could possibly be.

I proceeded through the program and was given more responsibility each month. By the second month we were helping prep and prepare meals for the restaurant. I moved from the Compass Center to another shelter with slightly better accommodations. The William Booth Center also allowed its clients more freedoms and autonomy than the Compass Center where the clients were expected to follow more house rules. By the third month we were able to set up the buffet stations in the restaurant and man the pasta and salad stations that made fresh, made to order, dishes for each customer. By the fourth month I'd moved into a four bedroom house that I shared with 2 other men and I was working side by side with guest chefs who came in once a week, on Thursday evenings, to prepare a four course meal for the public. This was one of Farestart's main fundraisers and it provided a large portion of the funding for the program. This evening was called Guest Chef Night and the guest chefs came from all of the great restaurants in the Seattle area. The chef donated the food for the meals and then came with a couple of members from their staff and worked alongside the Farestart students to prep and cook the meals. The meals were served by different community groups who volunteered each week and all tips and proceeds went to the program. This was also when graduates of the program received their diplomas and a gift of chef's knives that they could use in their new career. There was a new class starting almost every week so there was usually a graduation every Thursday evening. In my fourth month of the program I was offered a job at the Union Square Grill after working with the executive chef during Guest Chef Night. When I completed Farestart in February of 1999 this was the only restaurant that I applied to and I was hired immediately.

A lot occurred while I was in the program, both in my life and in the lives of my family members. My brother Doobie went to jail in the spring of 1997 for a drug offense and while I was at Farestart he was transferred to a work release program. Doobie was sentenced to two years but he qualified for the same W.E.C. program that I completed. Unfortunately after about a month in the program he kicked someone in the butt during an altercation and broke the dudes butt bone. He was kicked out of the W.E.C. program and had to do his entire two year sentence. I visited him at work release and took him money and clothing and looked forward to the day he would be released.

I also lost my cousin Michael Randolph Ealy while I was at Farestart.

Mt. Calvary held a New Year's Eve watch service every year so that the congregation would have a safe and enjoyable place to ring in the New Year without having to participate in the partying and revelry associated with New Year's outside of the church. I was at this service on December 31st 1998 when my cousin Jovan told me that Michael had been killed a few days earlier. Michael was out one night and for some reason called 911 because he wasn't feeling well. When the EMTs arrived they checked him out but Michael decided that he didn't want to be admitted and tried to leave. Police officers arrived on the scene and in the process of trying to restrain Michael applied some holds that caused him to stop breathing. The EMT personnel tried to revive him and rushed him to the hospital but he died. My aunt retained a lawyer but the officers were cleared of any wrong doing at a hearing. My aunt was not satisfied with the outcome and formed the Michael Randolph Ealy Foundation to fight police brutality and police corruption.

Not everything that happened while I was in Farestart was bad.

On Christmas day, December 1998, I proposed to Meko and she said yes. We were having Christmas dinner at her grandmother's house when I popped the question. Before proposing to Meko I asked her dad if I could have his daughter's hand in marriage. Although he laughed at my request, he said yes. After dinner I got down on one knee in front of all of her family and began to read some thoughts that I penned. Meko's aunt, Miss Carr, came over and took the paper from me and told me that I didn't need any notes because my proposal should come from the heart. Miss Carr was my English teacher my freshman year in high school so I'd known her longer than I'd known Meko. She was one of my favorite teachers and I respected her greatly so I reached down in my heart and told Meko how much I loved her and how wonderful it would be if she agreed to be my wife. Meko said yes and just like that we were engaged. We eventually set a date for July 17th 1999 and we began planning the wedding.

When I graduated from Farestart I had a job at Union Square Grill and a part time job at a gym downtown. I started working in the dish pit and gradually worked my way to a prep cook position. I began saving money and after a few months I had enough money to rent a house. I rented a two bedroom house in the Madison Valley area and moved Meko and Milan in. I didn't move in with them because I was not going to live with Meko until after we were married. The day Pastor Witherspoon prayed for me I not only gave up drugs, alcohol, and street life but I also gave up fornication. A lot of people didn't think it made sense to wait since we already had a child together but I wanted to make sure that I did everything the right way and I wanted to be obedient to what I thought God wanted me to do. So Meko and Milan lived in the house for about a month and I rented a room with Meko's uncle while we finished preparing for the wedding.

On July 17th 1999 Meko and I were married at Mt. Calvary Christian Center. Pastor Witherspoon officiated and my brother Doobie was my best man. Meko's matron of honor was her friend Jennifer and our wedding party was full of our friends and family members. It was a beautiful day that I spent loving my wife and appreciating my family. Before the service I ran around making sure everything went as planned and everybody was present and accounted for. The day was a little stressful with Meko's dress not being what she ordered and my brother Doobie seeming to go out of his way to irritate me, but Meko was able to purchase a new dress at the last minute and Doobie calmed down and started acting right after Meko grabbed hold of his bottom lip during pictures and told him to behave. It was her day and I did everything I could to make sure she was happy. She was in my corner through thick and thin and I loved her for that. Now I wanted to be the man that I knew she deserved. Meko looked beautiful walking down the aisle and I remember the joy I felt and the hope I had for our future.

The day after our wedding Meko and I went to brunch with several of our friends and family members and further celebrated our union. After brunch we went home to our house in the Valley and I carried her over the threshold of our house. I felt a swell of pride for enduring and doing it the way I believe God would have had me do it and we quickly settled into married life. Our future was bright and we were happy.

Three months later I celebrated my one year sobriety birthday and Meko shocked me by throwing me a surprise party and sending me to Washington DC for T.D. Jakes' Manpower conference. She talked to my job to get me time off work and made all the travel arrangements without me knowing. I almost cried when I found out. This was one of the nicest things anyone had ever done for me. I was very happy and I thanked God for my wife and her love for me.

DC was amazing and the conference was powerful. I was more and more involved in church at Mt. Calvary so I was overwhelmed by the presence of God I felt while worshiping in the DC stadium with thousands of other men of God. When I arrived in DC I ran into a few other Mt. Calvary men so I hung out with them a little but I spent most of my time seeing the sites between worship services. I also hung out with a cat from Seattle named Art who was there for the conference. Art killed a dude in Seattle a few years back and did some time in prison before being released on appeal. Art found God at some point during his incarceration but I was surprised and impressed by how genuine his love for God was now that he was out of jail. He and I went to some of the monuments and talked a lot about how good God was and all the different ways that He blessed us. I returned home on fire for God. I was committed to doing God's will and I was becoming more and more familiar with the bible and ministry. I joined the street ministry at church and I began to help out with the children's ministry. Life was good but I didn't know that soon I would face a major test that threatened everything that I'd worked for over the last year.

My brother Doobie was trying to get established back in society after getting out of prison but he was having a hard time finding a job and staying out of trouble. He was dating a girl he met and he was staying with her off and on as he tried to get himself back on his feet. One night he called me to talk to me about how hard it was to deal with his girlfriend sometimes while he was trying to stay positive and out of trouble. I listened to him for a long time, hearing the pain in his voice and understanding the struggle to stay positive when all he knew and was used to was street behaviors.

"You need Jesus," I said after listening to him for a while.

"What?" He replied.

"You need Jesus," I repeated. "You need to surrender your life and stop trying to do things the way you used to do them because they won't work."

I could hear my brother quietly sobbing on the phone so I continued.

"We are meant to be doing more than we've been doing. God loves us and created us to be positive manifestations of His love here on earth. I know its hard Doobie but you need to stop trying to do it your way and trust that God will guide you in a direction where you will be able to live a life of joy and peace."

"I know," he said in almost a whisper, "but how."

"First you need to accept Jesus Christ as your Lord and Savior and then God will begin to work in you to remove those things in your life that are hindering you from being who you are meant to be."

"Will you pray the prayer of salvation with me," I asked.

"Yeah," he said, "Let's do it."

I led my brother in the prayer of salvation and he accepted Jesus Christ as his Lord and savior and submitted his life to the care and guidance of God Almighty. After the prayer I was overwhelmed with a feeling of happiness so I began to worship and thank God crying "Hallelujah" and "Blessed be the name of God."

My brother and I talked for a while longer and I could hear the relief in his voice as we talked after the prayer. I told him that he should start reading the Gospel of John and read a chapter of Proverbs in the morning and a chapter from Psalms at night. I told him to find a church where he felt comfortable and he was challenged to study the bible and I told him to pray whenever he needed to make a decision and trust God to guide him. I told him I loved him and God had his back now so everything would be ok.

We got off the phone and I fell to my knees to thank God some more for saving my brother. A few weeks later I was surprised to see Doobie at Mt. Calvary on Sunday morning and I knew that God had begun a good work in him.

A couple of months after getting married I left my job at the Gym and took a job at a restaurant in the neighborhood called Philadelphia Fevre. Philadelphia Fevre was a family owned restaurant that served hoagies and cheese steaks. I was hired as a cook and worked alongside the manager and his wife. I still worked full time at the Union Square Grill so I just worked here about four hours a day.

From day one I noticed that the manager was a jerk. He yelled and cussed at his wife and stormed around the place like he had a permanent bad attitude. The manager didn't own the place he just ran it for the owner who purchased it from a lady from Philadelphia. This lady owned and operated the restaurant for years before selling it and moving back to the East coast. I worked the grill and helped serve the customers while the manager's wife worked the cash register and took orders. While we were doing this the manager ran around complaining and barking orders. I enjoyed the customers and the manager's wife was nice but it took all of my patience and self-control to keep from punching the manager in the face when he came around the corner cussing about this or that. One day I pulled him to the side during a slow period and told him that I would appreciate it if he did not curse or yell when communicating with me. He seemed to receive what I was saying but he continued to yell and cuss at his wife.

I continued working two jobs during October and November of that year and celebrated Thanksgiving with my family at my cousin's house. I hung out with my family like family does on holidays not knowing that this would be the last time I saw my brother Doobie alive.

On December 12th 1999 Meko and I came home from church and were just getting settled when I saw my friend Brian pull up in front of the house. When I saw him pull up I went out and stood on my porch as he got out of his car. As he walked around the car I saw that he was crying. I knew his dad had been ill lately so I immediately thought that something must have happened to his dad. I came off the porch and went down to the sidewalk to meet him.

"Marty, Doobie is dead." He told me.

"What?" I said.

"They found Doobie dead." He said through his tears.

"NOOOOOOOOOOOOOOO!!!!!" Meko came out on the porch in time to hear Brian tell me that my brother was dead and now she was yelling.

"NOOOOOOOO!!!!!!!!! It's not true" I heard her yell as I tried to understand what Brian was saying.

"How do you know," I asked wanting to believe that this was just some kind of hood rumor and my brother was ok.

"Jamal saw it and told the Kilgores," Brian said.

"Where is Jamal? Let's go find Jamal," I said as I got into Brian's car.

Brian and I drove by Jamal's house and I saw that there was police tape around the house. We then went back to the valley and were driving around when we saw Jamal walking down the street crying with his shirt off.

"Jamal" I yelled out the window as we pulled up alongside him. "get in."

Jamal hopped in the car and we began driving as he told me what happened.

The previous night Doobie ran into Jamal and Jamal's roommate Bijon at a club downtown. Doobie left the club with Jamal, Bijon, and a few girls and they went back to Jamal's house to hang out. Around three in the morning Jamal and the girls left and Doobie decided to sleep on the couch. Jamal was at his girlfriend's house when he got a call from Bijon's girlfriend. Bijon called his girlfriend to come over about the time that Jamal left. She said when she got to the house she saw someone in all black in the driveway. She was too scared to go in so she drove around the block. When she came around the second time the person was gone so she went into the house where she found Bijon on the couch dead from a gunshot wound and Doobie on the floor dead from four gunshots to his back. She ran out of the house and called Jamal who came to the house and confirmed that Bijon and Doobie had been killed.

Even after hearing Jamal tell me what he saw I still didn't believe my brother was dead. Jamal gave me the name of the detective who came to the house when he called 911 and Brian dropped me off downtown so that I could go to the detective's office. The detective showed me pictures of Doobie but it didn't look like my brother. It was not until I saw my brother in the morgue that I knew it was Doobie. My brother had a tattoo of a Tasmanian devil holding a shotgun on his right arm. It was original artwork that he created so when I saw the tattoo I knew my brother had been killed.

I broke down in the morgue and for a while I was inconsolable. I was angry and I thought about revenge. I didn't understand why this would happen after my brother accepted Christ. I was under the impression that God would protect him and walk him out of the lifestyle that he was trying to leave. I wasn't mad at God but I didn't understand what was going on. The next few days I spent a lot of time in prayer and meditation before I understood that God truly works in mysterious ways so He doesn't always do what makes sense to us.

I eventually came to realize that if I sought revenge it would be impossible to have a positive result. If I found the killers and killed them then I would be depriving someone else of a family member and causing someone to feel the pain my family and I were feeling. I didn't want some other children to have to go through what my niece and nephews would have to go through because of the death of their father. I also had to consider going to prison and leaving my family fatherless if I was caught seeking revenge. If I didn't go to prison there was the chance that I could end up dead. Either way, I could end up leaving my family fatherless and that's not something I was willing to do. I saw a cycle of violence that I refused to participate in. I thanked God for His presence in my life because I knew that five or ten years earlier my reaction would have been more reckless. After much prayer and many tears I left the problem of my brother's killer in God's hands knowing that He could handle it better than I.

We buried my brother on December 20th 1999. The service was held at Mt. Calvary and the church was packed to capacity with standing room only. My brother was loved by most of the people who knew him. He was crazy but likable. He was known for doing the erratic and unexpected but he was often the life of the party and he was a good friend to have. I released my brother to God's care knowing that he would be better off away from the troubles and tribulations that the rest of us would continue to struggle with. I spoke at the service and asked those who loved Doobie to make this a better world for his children. I appealed to all of them to live lives that were positive always considering the affects our actions would have on those around us. I told them that, unfortunately, to late I realized that I am my brother's keeper and we should all seek to live lives that bring God glory by fleeing negativity and embracing those positive thoughts, actions, and behaviors that lead to life. Several young men gave their lives to Christ that day and I realized that this might be the way that God chose to use my brother.

I quit my job at Philadelphia Fevre after my brother was killed. I knew that God was in charge of my brother's situation but I didn't trust myself to remain calm if the manager said or did something to upset me.

After graduating from Farestart I'd kept in contact with many of the staff so it was a wonderful reunion when I accompanied the Union Square Grill chefs for Guest Chef Night a year after my graduation. The local news even did a story on me and the

Farestart program. For a couple days cameras followed me around at work and then they filmed our dinner at guest chef night. It was good to be able to tell people about the good work Farestart was doing for people. The program made a huge difference in my life and I was sure that it was a valuable commodity in the effort to rehabilitate people who wanted to become valued members of society. I believed in the program so much I became a spokesman for a while.

Before my brother was killed Meko and I found out that we were expecting. Weeks before we found out that Meko was pregnant I'd had a dream that I would have a son. After the dream I told Meko that our son's name would be Maiz Imani, which means, delivered by faith. His name would represent how God brought me out of a destructive lifestyle through faith in God's power and love. After Milan's premature birth the doctors were concerned that Meko might not be able to carry the baby for nine months. She also suffered another miscarriage a couple months after our wedding so we were pretty concerned when we found out she was pregnant again. To alleviate this concern she had a special procedure that would allow her to carry the baby to term and not go into premature labor. When she was around five months pregnant we found out that we were having a boy. The following Sunday I danced around the church worshiping God and giving Him praise and honor for blessing Meko and I with a son. Maiz was born in July of 2000 and Meko and I were overjoyed at the beautiful addition to our family.

Before Maiz's birth I found us a bigger home on First Hill. Meko didn't want to move at first but she was happy when she saw the new place. It was closer to downtown so I was able to walk to work and there was a fenced in courtyard with a playground for the children.

I left Union Square Grill that year and took a job making a little more money working in an antique furniture showroom. I stayed there for a few months before being offered a job managing one of Farestart's cafes. I took the job with Farestart and began overseeing the everyday operations of two of their satellite restaurants. I also went to Washington DC to speak before congress about the need for more funding to support programs like Farestart.

I was still very active at Mt Calvary and was now a part of the security team. I was also taking classes to become a deacon. Pastor Witherspoon chose a group of men and asked us to consider becoming deacons so I was honored by his consideration and committed fully to the training. Around this time I learned that my sister was struggling. One Sunday I went out to visit her and was shocked to find that a group of Crips were using her house as a dope spot. I talked to the landlord of the house that we moved out of and he agreed to let her move in. I helped her and her son Malik move to the Valley and I felt a lot better after she got settled.

After a year on First Hill Meko and I moved in with her grand-mother so Meko could take care of her. One day I was on the bus headed to work when Meko called me on my cell phone to tell me that a plane crashed into one of the World Trade Center towers. When I got to work I turned the radio on just in time to hear the announcer reporting that another plane just crashed into the second tower. We didn't have a television in the shop so we played the radio all day and talked to the customers about what was going on in New York. I turned on the television as soon as I got home and watched as the news channels showed the crashes and collapse of the towers over and over again.

Malia came to live with us for a while so we moved into an apartment that could accommodate all of us. My sister was having trouble raising Malik so she agreed to let him stay with Meko and I until she got back on her feet. We stayed in our apartment for a year and then moved into another house in the Central District. I'd been ordained as a deacon and I was now also head of security acting as Pastor Witherspoon's personal bodyguard. Philadelphia Fevre was under new management so they asked me to come back as the manager working under a dude named Ben who would function as the executive manager. I accepted the job and returned to Philadelphia Fevre.

Ben was the cousin of the owner and he was from Philadelphia so he was somewhat of an expert on the topic of cheesesteaks and Tastycakes. Ben had a big east coast personality, a thick Philly accent, and he loved to talk about all things Philadelphia. I enjoyed working with Ben. We played chess during slow moments and, although he was very good, over time I began to get a few victories here and there.

After a few months on the job I began to think about how to increase sales and decided to host an open mic poetry night once a week. I got it started with a girl from Mt. Calvary and before we knew it Saturday nights were packed at the Fevre. I offered food and drink specials and ended up increasing sales to record highs.

My family and I were doing well, I had almost five years clean and sober, and I was doing well at my job. I should have known it was about time for another trial.

One day Meko received a call from the Everett coroner. When I got home from work she told me my dad had died.

It was November of 2003.

My dad went bowling and when he started feeling ill on the way home he stopped by a friend's house and asked if he could sleep on the couch. The next morning his friend found that my dad died in his sleep during the night..

I rushed out to the morgue in Everett and identified my dad. I then went by his friend's house to pick up his keys and some other personal items that she held onto instead of sending them with the EMTs. Then I called my oldest brother Speedy in Chicago to tell him the news. Speedy and I had the same dad but different mothers. I also had two sisters in Chicago named Merle and Tanya who had the same dad as me but different mothers. Speedy's real name was Carl, so my dad's name was Carl and I had two brothers named Carl. Speedy and I talked about what needed to be done and we set about planning my dad's funeral service. I contacted my job and let them know that I would need some time off and Ben told me to take as much time as I needed. I made arrangements to ship my dad's body back to Chicago while Speedy and my siblings in Chicago made the arrangements for the church and funeral home on that end.

I went to my dad's house to secure everything and I had to tell Jeff, Barb's son, that he had to find another place to stay while we settled my dad's estate. My dad and Barb were no longer together but Jeff and my brother Terrance still lived with my Dad. Terrance went to stay with Barb and I began the process of settling my Dad's estate.

Before I could really deal with the estate we had to bury my dad. I flew to Chicago with Meko, Malia, Milan, Malik, and Maiz. My sisters Sheila and Tash came as well. My family and I stayed with Speedy and Sheila and Tash stayed with another one of my family members. One of my cousins was married to a pastor so the funeral service was held at their church. It was a nice service and I cried when I thought about my dad and how we became closer over the last few years. He and I settled the differences that led me to move out years prior to his death so he would often come out to our house on the weekends to hang out with us and his grandchildren. Maiz loved him and they would sit around laughing and playing for hours. I'm not sure if Maiz understood the funeral service, because he was only three and a half years old, but he began to cry when he saw my dad and was unable to go to him. After the service we hung out with my Chicago family for a few more days reminiscing over days long gone and then my Seattle family and I returned home.

My dad created a living trust a few years before he died and made Speedy, my sister Merle, and I trustees. All of his affairs were already in order so all we had to do was contact the lawyer who facilitated the transaction and track down my dad's bank accounts and insurance policies. I took a couple of weeks off work and cleaned and remodeled my dad's house so that we could sell it. I hired a few dudes and we did all of the work ourselves. After selling the house and settling with the insurance companies all of my dad's children were left with a little bit of money. I told Ben that I wouldn't be coming back to Philadelphia Fevre and I started my own business.

I began flying to New York, purchasing clothing, and flying back to Seattle to sell them. This was when football and basketball jerseys were popular in the hood. I flew out to New York, purchased jerseys for $15 apiece and then sold them for $75 to $100 in Seattle. At first I sold them piece by piece and then I sold them in bulk to about four or five people who were selling for me. My business was doing well so Meko and I bought a house in south Seattle. We would have preferred a house in the central district but the houses in that area were way too expensive for us. I sold clothing for about six months until I realized that I either needed to open a store or do something different. I really didn't want to open a store so I decided to do something different.

In New York I'd reestablished some of my P.A. contacts so I began do production assistant work again. Since I now had experience in the food industry I was also able to find work in Craft Services. When I had work I'd stay in New York, for anywhere from a few weeks to a couple of months until, the project was completed, and then I would return to Seattle. I did various jobs in the film industry and was even Kim Field's assistant for three weeks while she directed a poetry project for one of the Viacom channels. In New York I'd stay with Chelsea and Jamie or my friend Anton who lived in Queens. I did this for about nine months until the time away from my family became too difficult to handle.

I returned to Seattle for good and did a couple of different jobs before I was injured while working on a construction site. I received compensation for my injury so I didn't have to work while I went to chiropractor for physical therapy.

Over time I began to realize that none of these occupations provided me with a sense of purpose. I recognized that I was just working and I believed God had something more for me than what

I was doing. I also wasn't as focused in the church as I had once been. We had left Mt. Calvary when we moved out of the Central district and although I was hungry for something more spiritually I wasn't sure what it was.

On October 30th of 2006 I relapsed and went on a three day drug binge. The 10th anniversary of my mom's death triggered anger, sadness, and frustration within me. I was removed from the church and all of the things that helped me deal with the various trials and tribulations of life so I was not equipped to handle the immense feeling of depression that I felt. Fortunately, I was able to snap back pretty quickly so I immediately checked myself into a detox facility for evaluation. I was in detox for about a week spending most of my time in prayer seeking answers to some nagging questions that were troubling my spirit. Day after day I would wake up with James 1:8 in my mind, which reads, 'A double minded man is unstable in all his ways.' After much prayer and quiet meditation I realized that I was running from God's calling on my life and I needed to surrender 100% to God's will. I realized that although I was active in the church I was still reluctant to release myself fully to do whatever God willed for me to do. No jobs were fulfilling to me because I wasn't meant to do just any job. I was created to serve God through ministry and He brought me out of the street so that I could be instrumental in helping someone else overcome the struggles I endured. For the first time in my life I understood fully what God desired of me. I knew he loved me when I received Christ, I knew he empowered me when I received the Holy Spirit, I knew he wanted me to serve Him when He delivered me from crack addiction, but it wasn't until now that I knew he wanted me to minister to His people. This was a scary thought because I had no idea what it would mean to give myself to God totally, but that day I surrendered. I fell to my knees and told God to have His way with me and guide me in His will. I submitted everything to God not knowing where I would end up.

One day I sat down to really meditate on my life. I decided that I wanted to create a legacy of promise for my children and that I wasn't going to end up dead or in jail. I wanted to become someone who was an asset to the society in which I lived and a benefit to the world community. I started to look more closely at my environment and question societal norms in an attempt to understand why some people were homeless while others had more money and resources than they could ever use. I wondered why there were more drug dealers than college graduates in the neighborhoods where I, and most of my friends, grew up. I became more sensitive to the injustice, inequality, and despair I witnessed and devoted my life, my skills, and my efforts to helping others, and in doing so, helping myself.

When I got out of detox I got a tattoo of James 1:8 on the inside of my right forearm to remind me to stay focused on doing the will of God.

For the next few days I struggled with what to do and where to go. Proverbs 3:5-6 came to me over and over. It reads, 'Trust in the Lord with all your heart and lean not on your own understanding. In all your ways acknowledge Him and He shall direct thy path.' I was being instructed to trust God and not worry about my situation. I went and got Proverbs 3:5-6 tattooed on the inside of my left forearm and I decided that these would serve as my blinders to keep me looking straight ahead and focused on God.

I entered a recovery/discipleship program and began to pray and fast while seeking spiritual direction. Soon a third scripture began to wake me up at night. Luke 4:18-19.which reads, 'The Spirit of the Lord is upon me, for He had anointed me to preach the gospel to the poor. He has sent me to heal the broken hearted, to preach deliverance to the captive, and recovery of sight to the blind. To set at liberty them that are bruised, to preach the acceptable year of the Lord.' When I heard this scripture in my head I wasn't so eager to embrace its message for it meant that I would be tasked with the responsibility of preaching the gospel. Becoming a preacher was the last thing that I wanted to do. Not only did I not want to carry the weight of the gospel but I knew how preachers were viewed by cats in the streets. But then I realized that that was why I was being called, so that, coming from the streets, I could reach some of those who were still in the streets. I stayed in the program for a month and when I got out I got Luke 4:18-19 tattooed on my left shoulder to remind me of my calling and purpose.

I didn't feel led to immediately begin preaching. Instead I felt the strong urge to go back to school and study the word so that I would be prepared when God decided to release me into my ministry.

First I enrolled in a small bible college in south Seattle. After four months I received an associates and a bachelor's degree from this school but it wasn't an accredited university and I wanted an education that would prepare me for whatever I might face in ministry. I began to consider other education options.

I returned to Farestart and was hired as an outreach coordinator and a case manager. I was responsible for recruiting students to the program and managing a caseload of students. My recruitment duties took me to homeless shelters, prisons, addiction recovery programs, and the back alleys of Seattle; ironically, all of the places where I had once found myself during my struggles with addiction and hopelessness. But this time when I hit the streets it was to bring positivity and help people combat hopelessness. This work awakened within me the overwhelming desire to seek God while living a life of service to the marginalized. My life experience and my encounters with the homeless, the addicted, and the incarcerated, gave me an appreciation for all people and a desire to see everyone receive the needed assistance and resources to help better their situations. This was right in line with where I felt God was taking me. My job was ministry and I was able to connect people in need with a program that I knew worked because it had worked for me. I went to prisons, shelters, rehab facilities, and street corners telling people about the program and inviting them to the Tuesday orientation. I was back on the block, but I was no longer a slave to a destructive lifestyle, instead I was an ambassador for change encouraging those I encountered to live whole. After a couple of months I was giving a caseload of students to manage and a life skills class to facilitate. I enrolled in classes at the community college in the fall and continued to work at Farestart while going to school.

By the end of the year I told Meko I wanted to go to school full time. She wasn't happy but she eventually got behind me. Farestart didn't want to adjust my schedule so that I could go to school so I resigned. I formed the Young Men's Institute and began facilitating workshops for at risk youth. I also helped a friend start a church near Pacific Highway in south Seattle. I preached my first sermon at this church and was licensed as a minister.

Due to my life experience there has been a gap of several years in my educational path. As a parent and husband it was necessary for me to provide for my wife and our children. I was responsible for keeping a roof over their heads, clothes on their backs, and food in their bellies. These efforts required much of my time and energy and I did not imagine that I would be granted another opportunity at higher education. However, I realized that continuing my education was necessary to acquire the resources, opportunities, and information that would make my service to others most affective. I enrolled at Seattle Central Community College full time in the fall of 2008 and decided to diligently apply every effort to obtain educational excellence in all of my scholarly endeavors.

At Seattle Central Community College I learned that I could obtain an Associate's degree in three quarters. So I took three classes the first quarter, four classes the second quarter and five classes the third quarter working hard to obtain my Associates degree within one year. In spite of this heavy work load I was able to maintain a 3.5 grade point average and become a member of the Phi Theta Kappa Honors Society. I also took the time to examine my goals and life interests to determine the career in which I would be most comfortable and effective. I knew that I was passionate about social service but I found that theological studies appealed to me as well. I found that although psychology and history were interesting, I really enjoyed studying about God, faith, service, and religious beliefs. This knowledge and my life experiences helped me to discern God's calling in my life, leading me to devote my energies toward developing my relationship with God and serving others as a result of that relationship. I have come to love and trust God and truly understand the importance of seeking His guidance in everything I do. It is also through this relationship that I have learned the value of knowledge and the importance of education. Hungry for wisdom and understanding, I began to ask deeper questions about life, society, and religion.

In January of 2009 we celebrated Barak Obama's presidential victory with an inaugural day party at our house. Several friends and family members came over to eat and watch the inauguration on TV and talk about how much it meant to have an African American president. I graduated from Seattle Central Community College with honors in June of 2009 and received my Associate of Arts degree. I was accepted into Seattle University and received a partial scholarship for being in the honors society. Over the summer of 2009 I worked with a mentoring program and went on a 40 day fast seeking guidance and direction from God. I went three weeks drinking only water, two weeks drinking water, juice, and broth, and five days drinking fluids and eating fruits and vegetables. This was a time of spiritual challenge and growth for me and although it was difficult I found that I could do a lot more than I expected when I put my full trust in God.

In the fall of 2009 I enrolled in Seattle University as a Theology and Religious Studies major and began a more in depth study of religion, spirituality, and faith seeking understanding.

Chelsea and Doobie 7/17/1999

Doobie on my wedding day

Doobie, Dad, & Me

Me, July 17th 1999

Meko & I on our wedding day

Milan, Maiz, & Malia

Maiz

Milan, Maiz, & Malik

Me, Doobie, & Neil

Doobie's funeral

Reverend Witherspoon at Doobie's funeral

Me and Doobie's pallbearers: Alvedo, Jamie, Kieth, DoRight, Jamal, & Neal

Chapter 8

EDUCATION REVISITED

*A wise man will hear and, and will increase
learning; and a man of understanding shall attain
unto wise counsels*
Proverbs 1:5

M y arrival at Seattle University was marked with both excitement and angst. I wondered if I would be able to excel at this institution and I didn't want to disappoint my family and those who I had convinced that returning to school at the age of 40 was a good idea. I participated in the Office of Multicultural Affairs' new student orientation with the hope of creating a sense of community that I didn't experience at Seattle Central Community College. We spent two days getting to know one another and playing introduction games. By the end of the orientation I'd made several new friends and I was ready to begin my studies. I can recall the butterflies in my stomach as I walked on the campus as a Seattle University student for the first time. The pride I felt when I purchased my textbooks and my Seattle University sweatshirt, and the anticipation of the first day of classes.

Along with the required core courses, I chose classes that I believed would complement my career choice. I registered for

Philosophy of the Human Person, Church as Community, and Early Christian Theology in the fall of 2009. I quickly found myself confronted by names, and ideas that were foreign to me. My Philosophy professor exposed me to Socrates, Plato, and Descartes and required me to meditate on existential theories and philosophical arguments that caused me to question, prove, and reassemble my faith. My Early Christian Theology professor introduced me to Aquinas, Augustine, Origen, and other church fathers. We spoke of the politics behind the church decisions and doctrines during its formation as the Universal Church, and I learned of those who were labeled heretics due to their challenges to certain ideas and doctrines. My decision to major in Theology was confirmed in my Church as Community class where I learned how the church, and the members of the church, should function in community with one another and those in need. We were encouraged to visit various places of worship and incorporate words like "commonality" into our understanding of Christian faith. These first classes at Seattle University showed me that there was much information left for me to acquire and stimulated my desire to learn more about the different ideas and manifestations of "faith."

I was quite disappointed when I received my grades for the first quarter and found that I received an A, a B+, and a B- resulting in a 3.3 grade point average. I worked hard and I thought that the grades I earned would be higher than they actually were. As I considered my grades I decided that this too was a lesson. I would work harder to insure that my work was worthy of the highest marks and that I was getting all of the knowledge the professors had to offer.

In the winter quarter of 2010 I enrolled in Philosophy of Ethics, the Hebrew Bible, and Medieval and Reformation Theology. These courses challenged my thinking and contributed to my desire to understand faith in action. In my Philosophy of Ethics class we struggled with the definitions of "morality" and "ethics." We entered into lively discussions around humankind's obligation to one another and debated about what actions were ethical or unethical and why. I was faced with the task of examining the premises on which I built my understanding of moral and ethical behavior and led to investigate the validity of my conclusions. It seemed as if the receptive capacity of my mind increased as new and vital ideas saturated my consciousness. It was also in this quarter that I learned to read the Hebrew bible from the perspective of the authors and the intended audience. We studied the culture and political situations in which the prophecies, stories, and historical accounts were written to gain new insight in understanding the reasons behind the stories. We studied the poetic characteristics of the original Hebrew texts and I decided that I must learn to read Hebrew and Greek so that I can read the bible in the languages in which it was written. Finally, there was my Medieval and Reformation Theology class. It was in this class where I was exposed to the theological revolution of Martin Luther and the doctrinal assertions of the Council of Trent. We studied Calvinism, Michael Himes, and the Roman Catholic response to the Protestant movements. I learned of the improprieties within the Universal Church during this period and the various challenges initiated by the lay people against ecclesiastical corruption, scandal, and spiritual blemish. We gained the ability to look at contemporary church policy and doctrine through new lenses. Through further study of the information shared in this class I began to question the absolute authority of the clergy within the church. This led me to explore issues of control and domination within the church under the guise of religion. Overall, my classes in this quarter were gratifying and I eagerly awaited the posting of the grades following finals week.

My grades for this quarter were two As and an A- which translated into a 3.9 grade point average. I felt like I was beginning to understand the expectations of the Seattle University professors and I aspired to do even better in the upcoming spring quarter.

By the spring of 2010 I'd adjusted well to student life at Seattle University. I was employed 15 hours a week in the Tekakwitha collegium and I worked 10 hours a week tutoring seventh and eighth graders at Washington middle school as part of the Children's

Literacy program. I was a member of the Seattle University rugby team and my studies were academically and intellectually rewarding.

For spring quarter I enrolled in Modern and Contemporary Theology, Spiritual Traditions East/West, and Music and Politics of the Black Diaspora. Of these three classes it was the latter that made the most lasting impression on me. In this course we studied the interaction and influence of African American entertainers in national and international politics during the cold war era. We listened to the music of Dizzy Gillespie, Lena Horne, Paul Robeson, Louis Armstrong, and Duke Ellington and discussed how these artists were used as peace ambassadors by President Eisenhower. We studied the international appeal of music and its effectiveness in breaking down global walls of division. We studied the history of African American forms of music and entertainment as they evolved from slavery to the Jim Crow era. We then examined how these forms of expression helped African Americans cope with the various forms of oppression they faced during these periods. During this class I began to look at the contemporary African American community and question the role of the African American church in the struggles for social, educational, and economic equality. I wanted to know how the African American church participated in community growth and development during the slavery, Jim Crow, and cold war eras, and how it was participating today. So after speaking with my advisor, I decided to research this question for the Departmental Honors addendum to my Theology and Religious Studies degree. I finished spring quarter with a 4.0 grade point average and I went into my summer break excited about returning to school as senior.

In the fall of 2010 I returned to Seattle University as a full time student while working thirty hours a week as an Outreach Worker for the YMCA. As an outreach worker I worked with at risk and gang involved youth. I helped them acquire resources for school and advocated on their behalf in the criminal justice system. We also facilitated fun activities to build relationships and trust. In November I passed my ordination exam which qualified me to become an ordained reverend in the Baptist church. My Ordination ceremony wouldn't be held until the spring of 2011 but I was excited about where God was taking me.

I enrolled in Biomedical Ethics, The Gospel of Jesus, and Latin American Liberation Theology. It was soon apparent that all three of these courses would be both challenging and enlightening. In the Biomedical course we looked at issues of ethics within the scientific and medical fields. We examined case studies where physicians in New Orleans, during hurricane Katrina, were charged with crimes after they systematically decided who would receive lifesaving treatments and who would not. We discussed the reasoning behind the doctor's decisions and debated about the ethical and moral responsibilities of doctors who take an oath to first do no harm. I decided to write a paper on the Tuskegee Experiments and investigate unethical and immoral behaviors in medical and scientific experimentation involving humans as case studies. My Biomedical Ethics studies were complimented by my studies in Latin American Liberation Theology. I learned of the marginalized people in Latin America and saw how government interests were often considered more important than the welfare of a country's citizens. Dr. Rodriguez and Jon Sorbino made me aware of the presence of marginalized people around the world. I was then challenged as a Christian to acknowledge the church's responsibility to participate in the people's struggle to obtain life giving resources and opportunities. ...the reign of God should be understood not just as beneficent action, but as liberating and as partisan, since oppressed people are- by right- at the center of God's regard and God's action. (Sobrino 2008)

It was here in Dr. Rodriguez's class that I realized that the spiritual lessons of Jesus were contingent not only on one's search for a spiritual creator, but also in the proper treatment and interaction with God's creation. Biblical scripture seemed to take on new meaning for me. I read and understood that Jesus' ministry opposed those who oppressed, yet served, fed, healed, and encouraged the poor, the sick, and the marginalized. This realization could not have come at a more opportune time. For it was at this time that I was also studying The Gospel of Jesus. The questions "who was Jesus" and "what was His message" seemed to synchronize perfectly with the investigation of the church's responsibility to the poor and marginalized. We looked at the life and words of Jesus and learned that humankind's just and loving treatment of one another was indispensable in the process of being reconciled with a just and loving God. Within me a dominant question began to emerge. Was I, as a singular disciple of Christ, and the Church as a collective, truly emulating the actions and ministry of Jesus? I would argue that as a collective we are not and as an individual there was much for me to learn in order to adequately further the true ministry, message, and mission of Jesus. Liberal Protestant theologians such as Adolf von Harnack worked to focus attention on how Jesus' teachings could be applied in contemporary societies free from the dogma of the church

Harnack emphasized that Christianity is a way of life, not a system of beliefs, dogma, or doctrine. Jesus proclaimed God as Father, the brotherhood and sisterhood of human beings, the infinite value of the human soul, and the "love commandment": to love God, ourselves, and other human beings, including our enemies. In other words, an authentic faith in Jesus does not consist in creedal orthodoxy but of doing what Jesus did. (Gowler 2007)

My studies began to increasingly influence my thoughts and actions outside of the classroom as I scrutinized myself, the church, and governmental policies. I was more aware of governmental acts of oppression and the social and political conditions of the populations that were being dominated. I became more perturbed by the marginalized people in Seattle. What could and should be done locally and globally to change the systems of oppression and domination so prevalent in our world? I decided that more study was necessary if I ever intended to be an effective agent of positive change. With these thoughts ringing in my mind the winter quarter of my senior year began.

In order to graduate in June, I was required to complete a senior synthesis class and the fourth and fifth classes of the 400 level theology series. I enrolled in Religion as Social Change and Theology of Religions then registered for "directed reading" to satisfy the research portion of my Departmental Honors project. Theology of Religions appealed to me because religious pluralism is one of the topics that I am most interested in. In this course we studied Christian theologians such as William James, Thomas Merton, and Karl Rahner, as well as the theological ideas of Talad Asad, a Muslim theologian. We were able to look at and discuss the worldwide differences in religious expression. We then attempted to determine what methods and criteria are used by different groups to legitimize doctrines, mystical experiences, and ideas of religious faith. This class planted the desire within me to study the Coptic Christians in Egypt, and the Christians in Ethiopia. I hoped to be exposed to the different expressions of Christianity beyond the Christian expression that has its roots, foundation, and formation in Rome and the Catholic Church.

With my curiosity once again peaked I entered my senior synthesis class to learn how to take all of the knowledge I attained and incorporate it into a paper. This paper would hopefully also illustrate how I would include the obtained information in my future thoughts and actions. My professor, Dr. Rodriguez, was an excellent adviser on how we should properly prepare an exceptional scholarly paper or essay. We were given the opportunity to receive feedback from our classmates and give suggestions on their writings. These exercises helped me to see the importance of clarity and the explanation of thoughts and ideas in effective writing.

It was also during this quarter that I had the opportunity to visit Wake Forest University at the invitation of the Wake Forest Divinity School Office of Admissions. After reviewing my application for admission into the Master of Divinity program at Wake Forest

Divinity School, the office of admissions determined that they would like for me to interview for their most prestigious fellowship, the Samuel Wait Fellowship. The Samuel Wait Fellowship, which is named in honor of Samuel Wait, one of the founding members of Wake Forest University, covers the entire cost of tuition for three years and provides a $10,000 stipend per year for living expenses.

I flew down to Winston-Salem, North Carolina, where I toured the campus and met students, faculty, and staff before my interview with the board. Due to my theological preparation at Seattle University I felt confident that I would be able to answer any theological or religious questions that the board might ask. The visit went wonderfully and I left the interview feeling as if the educational excellence available to Seattle University students had been well represented. A week later I was informed that although I did not receive the Wait Fellowship I did receive a scholarship that would cover the entire cost of tuition and fees and a $4000 stipend. This assistance would be in place for me for the three years necessary for me to complete my Master of Divinity requirements. I was overjoyed and overwhelmed by this opportunity and I am aware that none of it would have been possible without the educational preparation I received at Seattle University.

On February 22nd, 2011 I registered for my final quarter of study at Seattle University. I enrolled in Spanish 135, The Synoptic Gospels, and the writing portion of my Departmental Honors program. Joyfully I anticipated the forthcoming commencement ceremony in June and fought against the dreaded "senioritis" illness that has been known to overcome students in their senior year of study. With some trepidation I prepared for the final foreign language requirement for my degree. I had already taken two previous quarters of Spanish and I found it to be the most difficult course of study I had taken thus far. It was for this reason that I reserved this final course for my last quarter at Seattle University. I did not want a C grade, which is what I received in the prior two Spanish courses, to adversely affect my grade point average. Although I was somewhat nervous about the upcoming Spanish course, I was aware of how important it was for me to learn how to communicate in a language different than my own. I knew that if I were to truly serve the global community it would be necessary for me to speak the language of the communities I entered into. I knew that as I continued my academic track it would be necessary for me to learn to read and write in the Hebrew and Greek language for my Master of Divinity requirements. It would also be necessary for me to learn to read and write in French and German for my PhD studies and communicate in Amharic and Arabic if I traveled to Egypt and Ethiopia. It was with this in mind that I recruited fellow students more adept at the Spanish language than I to assist me in this daunting task.

My approach to my other two courses in this quarter was a bit more enthusiastic. I looked forward to continuing a critical and historical analysis of Jesus and His ministry in my Synoptic Gospel class, and my Departmental Honors writing and research was coming along smoothly. My Departmental Honors advisor, Dr. Sharon Suh, was extremely helpful in assisting me in the process of developing my thesis, researching the area of interest, and compiling a scholarly essay.

I look back over the time spent in study and community at Seattle University and I am optimistic about my personal future and the future of our global community. I have been privileged to participate in conversations with some of the world's great academic minds and watch as future great minds are shaped and formed. When I entered Seattle University I knew how important education was to me, yet, I now know how important it is for all of the world citizens to have equal opportunities to be educated to assist in the pursuit of human rights.

I now see how education can allow one access to resources necessary for social and economic stability. I also see how education can improve physical, mental, and emotional health. It is with this gained knowledge that I endeavor to be an impetus for social equality and spiritual growth in the communities that I encounter.

It is also with this knowledge that I decided that I would strive to continue my educational journey up to and beyond the doctorate level. As an African American male it is my opinion that more African American males should stress the importance of faith and education to our young people. I intend to be an educated voice doing so. I intend to work hard in all of my endeavors and I will not take any opportunities for granted. I intend to share the knowledge I receive with those who may not have access to the institutes of higher learning that I have been privileged to attend. Finally, I intend to give to others in honor of all those individuals who have graciously given to me. It is with both pride and humility that I recall my time at Seattle University and it is with sincere thanks that I remember all those in the Seattle University community who have contributed to my spiritual, social, and academic growth. I completed my degree requirements at Seattle University in June of 2011 and received my Bachelor of Arts Degree in Theology and Religious Studies. That spring I was also ordained as a Baptist minister under the tutelage of Reverend Aaron Williams, the senior pastor at Mount Zion Baptist Church in Seattle.

Convincing my wife Meko to move so that I could attend graduate school was quite a task. Meko supported me in most of my endeavors and she came to expect a sense of fluidity with me. However, this move was different. Meko and my children had never lived anywhere other than Seattle. They were all born, raised, and firmly rooted in the Evergreen State. In fact Meko had never been out of Seattle for longer than one week at a time. Her grandparents on her mom's side and her dad's side settled in Seattle decades ago and raised their families there. As a result, Meko had aunts, uncles, brothers, sisters. nieces, nephews, and cousins on both sides of her family residing in Seattle and it would be very difficult for her to leave them. This conversation could not have even been explored a few years earlier when Meko was caring for Gram. Meko was not willing to leave Gram and she became her caregiver after Gram had a stroke. When Gram passed Meko was

more willing to consider moving and we entered into the conversation of what a move of this magnitude would involve. Meko wanted
me to take the best financial offer available to me, which I did, and
she wanted a warm climate. I applied to Princeton, Yale, Vanderbilt,
Emory, and Wake Forest. I was accepted at Vanderbilt, Emory, and
Wake Forest. I received full tuition financial aid packages from all
three but I decided to accept an offer from Wake Forest Divinity
School where, after further consideration, I was awarded the Wait
Fellowship. After hearing the details of my financial aid package
and my plan for relocating us Meko finally agreed to the move.
We began the process of packing our belongings to be shipped
and selling or giving away everything we were not taking with us.
We sold both of our vehicles and all of our furniture then we were
ready to embark upon this next phase of our journey.

After making plans and taking care of all of the details we
postponed our departure when Meko's uncle Carl passed suddenly
from bladder cancer. We stayed for an additional week to attend
the service and spend time with the family and then Meko, Maiz,
and I boarded the plan to North Carolina with Milan planning to
come out about two weeks later.

We landed at the Greensboro airport in June of 2011 and made
our way to baggage claim where I found out that I was not able to
rent a car from the airport without a round trip ticket. We gathered
our bags and waited for a shuttle to take us to the apartment I
rented for us. When the shuttle arrived we stepped out of the
air-conditioned airport and we were immediately engulfed by the
warm humid North Carolinian climate. The shuttle driver took us to
our apartment complex where we met with the apartment manager
and received our keys. After leaving our bags in the apartment I
tracked down a rental car agency that would let me rent a vehicle.
We rented a vehicle, had a meal, and then began the process of
adjusting to life in Winston Salem.

We stayed in the apartment for about a month and a half before
we found a nice three bedroom house to move into within walking

distance of the school. During that month and a half we bought a little car to get us around town and took a trip to Mississippi for my family reunion. We stayed in Mississippi for about two weeks and then we returned to Winston Salem so that Milan, Maiz, and I could prepare for our upcoming school year.

Maiz adjusted well to the move while Milan struggled a bit early on. She was starting her senior year in high school and she had to leave all of her friends and start in a new high school where she didn't know anyone. This was one of the major concerns that Meko and I had regarding the move. Although we knew that the move was necessary in order to better equip ourselves for a prosperous and productive future we didn't want to harm our children in the process. Meko and I decided that we would keep a close eye on the children and support them in making this somewhat difficult life change. We are all in this together and I am grateful for the support I've received from my wife and children.

My classes at Wake Forest began in August of 2011 and I was excited to start. My first year I took courses in Hebrew, Christian Ethics, Homiletics, African American Theologies, Art of Ministry, and Old Testament. I had the opportunity to spend 12 days in Israel as part of a Christians, Jews, and Muslims in the Holy Land course. I was blessed to be able to walk where Jesus walked, wade in the Dead Sea, and watch a sunset over the Sea of Galilee. I also visited the tombs of the patriarchs, the garden of Gethsemane, and prayed at the Western Wall during the Sabbath. My second year I took courses in Greek, Urban Ministry, Pastoral Care, New Testament, Jewish Scrolls, and Christian Education. I also had to have surgery after tearing my pectoral muscle while bench pressing 425 pounds. The first two years of my three year program flew by and I am looking forward to the next leg of this life journey.

As I write this it is summer and I am preparing to begin my final year at Wake Forest. I have learned much throughout my life, in both the formal and informal classrooms. I know that I must remain close to God and live as if all of the moments of my life are precious and valuable. I cannot make up for the time I lost or remove my mistakes from the account of my life but I can learn from them and teach others to avoid the pitfalls that caused me to stumble. My life has taken quite a turn and I am extremely optimistic about my future. I have had the opportunity to survive a lifestyle that has been known to be deadly and destructive. By the grace of God I am alive while many of my friends and family members are not. I know that I do not deserve to be where I am and I know that I am here only because God has a purpose for my life.

I wrote this book because I know I have a responsibility to do all that I can to ensure the survival and wellbeing of our youth and communities. I wrote this book to help our young people learn from my mistakes and avoid making choices that will prevent them from becoming viable members of society who are able to benefit from all that this society has to offer. I wrote this book to encourage those who have fallen and show them that with determination and God's help you can overcome your mistakes and be the great person you were purposed to be. I wrote this book to tell my story so that my children know my portion of their history in the hopes that they will draw strength from their heritage and the legacy I leave them. I desire to be an encouragement to all who I encounter and a source of strength for those who are struggling with some of the obstacles I endured. I pray that my story provides hope to the hopeless. I pray that it strengthens the weary. And I pray that it gives new life to someone who is seeking a change and a better way of living. There is much work to be done to improve the condition of this world and it is my desire to be of service.

18 The Spirit of the Lord is upon me, because he hath anointed me to preach the gospel to the poor; he hath sent me to heal the brokenhearted, to preach deliverance to the captives, and recovering of sight to the blind, to set at liberty them that are bruised, 19 To preach the acceptable year of the Lord. Luke 4:18-19

My ordination

The Lawsons at my ordination

Family at my ordination

Javin, Meko, & Malik

Family at Mt. Zion

Family after church

AUTHOR BIOGRAPHY

R everend Martin L. Lawson was ordained at Mt. Zion Baptist Church in Seattle Washington in January of 2011.Reverend Martin L. Lawson completed the requirements for his Bachelor of Arts in Theology and Religious Studies/ with Departmental Honors at Seattle University and graduated Cum Laude in June of 2011. In the fall of 2011 Reverend Lawson began his studies at Wake Forest University School of Divinity as a Wait Scholar. He received his Master of Divinity degree from Wake Forest University School of Divinity in May of 2014. Reverend Lawson currently resides in Winston Salem, North Carolina with Meko, his wife of 14 years and his 13 year old son Maiz. Reverend Lawson is also the proud father of Milan and Malia, and grandfather of Makiya, Mika, and Mathew Jr.

BIBLIOGRAPHY

Gowler, David. The Historical Jesus. New York: Paulist Press, 2007.

Sobrino, Jon. "No Salvation Outside the Poor: Prophetic Utopian Essays." Maryknoll: Orbis Books, 2008.

CPSIA information can be obtained at www.ICGtesting.com
Printed in the USA
BVOW11s1600150114

341938BV00010B/486/P